SNYDER

N E W   Y O R K

For Frank & Kim Schlehr—
Enjoy this walk down
memory lane!

Julianna Fiddler-White
2009

SNYDER

NEW YORK

A BRIEF HISTORY

Julianna Fiddler-Woite

Charleston   London

THE
History
PRESS

Published by The History Press
Charleston, SC 29403
www.historypress.net

All images are from the author's collection unless otherwise noted.

First published 2009

Manufactured in the United States

ISBN 978.1.59629.639.8

Library of Congress Cataloging-in-Publication Data

Fiddler-Woite, Julianna.
Snyder, New York : a brief history / Julianna Fiddler-Woite.
p. cm.
Includes bibliographical references.
ISBN 978-1-59629-639-8
1. Snyder (N.Y.)--History. 2. Snyder family. I. Title.
F129.S6935F53 2009
974.7'97--dc22
2009001702

In memory of Robert C. Fiddler and Theresa C. Woitaszek
and dedicated to my children
Victoria Julianna
Wendy Melissa Anne
Laceyanne Elise and
Mitchell Snyder Woite
You are the future of the Snyder family

CONTENTS

CONTENTS

PREFACE

After a formal dinner, at which many of the guests were authors, a man said to a friend in confidence, "I can imagine one wanting to know an author after reading his book, but I cannot imagine anyone desiring to read a book after knowing its author."
—Amherst Bee, *June 7, 1883*

As the great-great-granddaughter of Snyder's namesake, Michael Snyder, I have always had a vested interest in preserving the history of Snyder, New York. At twelve years old, I wrote my first piece on Snyder's history and submitted it to Mr. David Kinnin, my seventh-grade social studies teacher at Amherst Junior High. The immediate spark of his interest was enough positive reinforcement to commit me to this project for a lifetime. While many authors are quick to acknowledge their inspiration for a given work, they often overlook the lasting impression they too leave behind. In 1997, following my first official publication about Snyder, I sent Mr. Kinnin a copy of the book and a thank-you note for his support over fifteen years prior. Much to my surprise, Mr. Kinnin responded with a vivid account of my time in his classroom, including a clear memory of the desk at which I sat as I penned my first Snyder "manuscript." It was then that I truly appreciated the magnitude of what I could accomplish and the memories I could create.

In the years since, I have relished any opportunity to inform listeners about the places and faces that have made Snyder the community it is today. Feeling like somewhat of a living artifact, I truly enjoy bringing my family's stories to the people of the community. Whether it is the smiles of schoolchildren as they see vintage images of familiar locations or the remembrances of adults who get the chance to live some of their favorite memories over again, the people of this area never disappoint. What has proved challenging, however, is that pesky fact that history is always growing. Almost daily, landscapes change or snow falls and history happens. Quite honestly, keeping up with all of this is wearing me out!

Hence, what we have here is my best attempt to chronicle Snyder's highlights from the early 1800s to the present. Many photographs, never before seen, are being published with this work. Thanks to the dusty photo albums of some of Snyder's best pack rats and a treasure-trove of images housed at the Snyder Fire Hall and Amherst Alumni Foundation, Snyder and its residents may be seen as never before. As you read along and study the images, my hope is that you will come to appreciate the hamlet of Snyder for both what it was and what it shall remain: a place for families. As part of the Snyder family, I officially welcome you to my hometown!

ACKNOWLEDGEMENTS

Thanks to all of you for enduring my millions of questions and crazy requests!

Amherst Alumni Foundation, Ellen Marshall and Chris Byrd
Amherst Museum
Caroline Duax
Lois Fiddler
Jim and Kathy McNeill
Brandy Retallack
Kim Retallack
Peter Scumaci
Dorothy and Bill Shaver
Snyder Fire Department, Chief Tom Merrill
Martin Quinn
and especially…
Rob, Mitch, Lacey, Wendy and Vicky Woite

CHAPTER ONE

THE EARLIEST DAYS

The New York Pioneers and the Snyders' Trip from Pennsylvania

THE FIRST SETTLERS

Any historic tale of the regions of Western New York would have to start with the Iroquois Indians and their sale of the Western New York frontier. Following the Treaty of Big Tree in 1897, the Indians relinquished their claim to the forest-clad land and received 2.5 cents per acre from New England–based financiers. After passing through a series of hands, 3,300,000 acres of Western New York were purchased by a collection of Dutch financiers known as the Holland Land Company. It was through these individuals that the settlement of the frontier began, as the company sold large plots to early pioneers.

One of the first to settle in the Snyder area was a prominent man by the name of Timothy S. Hopkins. Hopkins was born in Barrington, Massachusetts, on March 10, 1776, just four months prior to America's independence. By the end of the 1700s, Hopkins would follow his half brother, Asa Ransom, to New York State and the pair would settle in Clarence, where Timothy ran a small sawmill. In 1804, Hopkins purchased seventy-five acres of land in the desolate region of Amherst that would become Snyder.

The Hopkins property spanned much of the Main Street area between Amherst Central High School near Washington Highway and the Denny's Restaurant near Harlem Road. On this plantation, he erected a large log house in preparation for his marriage to Nancy M. Kerr. This simple log house is significant for two reasons. First, it was to this humble house that Timothy Hopkins brought his new bride after the first recorded marriage in Erie County. Furthermore, in the years that would follow, this residence would become the first true social center of the growing region. Although the house would change from log to stone, the strong relationship between the Hopkins family and their community would not vary. By 1811, Hopkins held the rank of brigadier general in the New York State Militia and served valiantly in the War of 1812. He would go on to become the first supervisor of the new town of Amherst in 1819 and serve as its justice of the peace for thirty-two years. After accomplishing many things in the military and the community, not to mention successfully raising nine children, the Hopkins family sold the Main Street estate to the Schenck family in 1830 and took up residence in Williamsville.

THE SNYDERS LEAVE PENNSYLVANIA

Abraham Snyder was born in Pennsylvania in 1797. A mere twenty years after the Revolution and the United States' independence, the world Abraham was born into was one of constant change and development. A year prior, John Adams had been elected president in the first contested election and Thomas Jefferson had assumed his role as vice president. Territorially, Tennessee had just become a state and many Americans were beginning to search beyond the New England territories for their homesteads. At this time, records indicate that the Snyder family resided in a "Pennsylvania Dutch" area near Lancaster and Dauphin Counties in eastern central Pennsylvania. It was here that Abraham met and married Veronica Schenck (1795–1884), who was two years his elder. At their wedding, Veronica wore a delicate white lace wedding shawl and both she and Abraham posed for individual wedding day tintype portraits. As a present from the families, the couple received a nine-foot-tall grandfather clock.

By 1823, James Monroe was president of the United States and his Monroe Doctrine outlined the country's opposition to foreign intervention. Nationally, hard times were increasing unemployment and numerous businesses were collapsing in bankruptcy. On the brighter side, the textile mills were expanding in New England and it seemed as if the entire United States was expanding as well. With a population of 638,453, America now boasted twenty-four states, and westward expansion was occurring at an alarming rate. In this year, Abraham and Veronica Snyder, who now had a two-year-old son, made a crucial decision of their own. They knew that a caravan of covered wagons was passing through Stony Creek and they had decided to join them. More than likely, the Snyders wanted to join Veronica's relations, the Schencks, in the region that would eventually bear their name. It is also possible, however, that the family had decided to travel toward Buffalo in an effort to capitalize on the profits of a growing city. Although the westward extension of the Erie Canal began in 1819, it was not until August 9, 1823, that digging began in Buffalo. As one can imagine, the Erie Canal was a tremendous draw for this region. Not only was there immediate work on the construction of the canal but also many business opportunities tied to the finished product. Between 1820 and 1840, the population of Erie County increased 145 percent and the Snyders were a part of this. Whether it was the promise of opportunity, family connections or personal reasons that drew the Snyders to this region, the impact of the decision would resonate for generations to come.

Hence, in 1823, Abraham and Veronica loaded their two-year-old son Michael (1821–1902) into a covered wagon, attached an ox-cart and headed north. As anyone who has ever tried to pack for a simple vacation can imagine, the days preceding this serious departure were accompanied by many pensive decisions. The Snyders not only had to pack enough food and supplies for their journey but also enough goods to help them start a new life in the North. Among the traditional items one might expect to find on a journey of this nature, there was one particular piece in the Snyders' luggage that stood above all others. Neatly packed among the family's necessities was a wedding present of not only enormous sentimental value, but of simply enormous proportions. As if in an attempt to bring all the familiarity and comforts of home, neatly secured in the Snyders' ox-cart was the nine-foot-tall, solid cherry grandfather clock. The presence of this clock among the Snyders' possessions indicates two things. First, the family not only planned on building a life in the North but also a house large enough to accommodate this clock. Second, Abraham and Veronica Snyder were loyal to all that they loved…no matter how inconvenient this loyalty may be.

In 1823, the Snyders' migration north was a truly brave and harrowing adventure. Much of the land between Stony Creek and Buffalo was thickened by woods or raised by mountains. Regardless of the weather or terrain, the caravan traveled steadily, gaining and losing participants along the way. Miraculously, throughout this journey there was only one tragedy on record for the Snyder family. In a near brush with destiny, the grandfather clock suffered a frightening tumble from the ox-cart. Suffering only minor bruises and one large crack down the body, the clock was cleared to regain the caravan in a matter of minutes.

With no further tragedy, the Snyder family and the nine-foot-tall clock arrived safely in the Western New York wilderness within the year. Amazingly, 185 years after this arrival, the Snyders' grandfather clock still stands as a constant reminder of the struggles and sacrifices of our earliest pioneers. Interestingly enough, in an effort to preserve the memories of these early struggles, the Snyder family never fixed the crack in the clock's body. Wishing to pay homage to the bravery and tenacity that the pilgrimage required, Abraham, Veronica and every generation of Snyders since have cherished the crack and the values it has come to represent. Thousands of patrons were able to marvel at both the size and folklore of this cherry wood clock, once on loan to the Amherst Museum. In 1995, however, Greg Hunt (Abraham and Veronica's great-great-great-grandson) finally bought a house tall enough to accommodate the clock and brought it back into the family fold.

A truly inspiring story of love and determination, the Snyders' journey north is a tale of epic proportions. It is fascinating not only because of the magnitude of the journey but also for the impact that this journey would have on the generations to come. This one event was not only the impetus for the creation of a hamlet called Snyderville, but it has brought to light one of the great morals of our time: never let tradition dictate what you put in your ox-cart.

THE SNYDERS' ARRIVAL

At the time of the Snyders' arrival, the forests covered most all of the region between Williamsville and the city of Buffalo. There was one dirt path, known as the "Great Trail," which connected Amherst to the growing city. Later, the Great Trail was deemed the "Buffalo Road" and eventually it was christened "Main Street." The young town of Amherst had been in existence since 1818 and most of it operated out of "Williams Mills," or Williamsville. The village, named for Jonas Williams, boasted a gristmill, sawmill, water mill, tavern, quarry and general store. The only true business in the village was a tannery operated by Jonas Williams, who also founded several of the running mills. Any houses resting between Williams Mills and the city of Buffalo were predominately log cabins, and most of these had been vacated by earlier frontiersmen. At this time, a typical cabin measured twelve by sixteen feet and was constructed mostly of small, bark-covered logs. Windows, like doors, were hinged pieces of bark and most floors consisted of firmly packed dirt. The elite cabin of the day may have extended to sixteen feet square with a shingle roof and split-log floor. A window, which commonly contained six panes of glass, was a sure sign of affluence. Inside the cabin, one would usually find a simple table and maybe some chairs and a feather bed. Usually, however, bedsteads and chairs were only owned by the higher classes. Depending on the circumstances surrounding a family's departure, incidentally, any or all of these belongings may have been found by the next family to inherit the cabin.

It was in one such log cabin that the Snyders decided to end their pilgrimage. Settling in a nearly desolate region between Williamsville and Buffalo, the Snyders became early residents of the village that now bears their name. As luck would have it, the cabin that the family found did contain a few necessities, including a lavish feather bed. This stranger's bed became an intricate part of the Snyder family. Before its retirement, two generations of Snyder children were born in this bed, and on it, most family members drew their last breath.

In addition to the Hopkins family, the Snyders also settled near their cousins, the Schencks. Leaving Pennsylvania just prior to the Snyders, the Schenck family arrived in Western New York in 1821, bringing with them two covered wagons and four horses. The family originally settled in a small log cabin on Main Street just east of Harlem Road until their son, John, bought the Hopkins property in 1830. With the arrival of the Snyders, the Schencks and the Hopkinses became part of an early neighborhood.

With the Schencks and the Hopkinses for neighbors, the Snyders settled into their new life. Throughout the 1820s, Abraham, it is understood, worked hard to provide for Veronica and Michael. Although predominately a farming family, the Snyders also dabbled in any venture that seemed lucrative, including selling trees from their property to the Buffalo Courthouse as firewood. Nationally, this period in time saw the development of the electric motor, the Colt six-shooter and the first American locomotive. Most importantly, however, as Noah Webster was breathing life into his first Webster's Dictionary, Veronica Snyder was giving life to the Snyders' second child. Hence, after eight years in the Snyder area, Veronica and Abraham Snyder welcomed their second son, Jacob, on December 12, 1831. For the new family of four, life and business were good.

CHAPTER TWO

THE BIRTH OF SNYDERVILLE

Michael Snyder Creates Business and Forms a Community

THE DISAPPEARANCE OF ABRAHAM SNYDER

Almost as if borrowed from the pages of a Sherlock Holmes novel, the birth of Snyderville may well be attributed to a most bizarre and tragic sequence of events. Were it not for the following, the village of Snyder may have evolved in an entirely different direction, or possibly not at all.

The period was the late 1830s, and excavation had just begun on an addition to a popular Williamsville restaurant. The restaurant, known as the Eagle House, was built in 1832 alongside a prominent stagecoach stop on the old Buffalo Road. During the early 1800s, travel by stagecoach was often looked upon as dangerous due to the seedy nature of the tavern stops along the way. In an effort to amend this, the Eagle House had been erected at the Williamsville stop. By the mid-1800s, the present restaurant was doing so well that the decision to extend the establishment farther to the rear had been made. It was during this process that a mystery began to unfold. While digging behind the original stagecoach stop, workers were greeted with a tragic surprise: the skeleton of a very unlucky traveler. After the body was exhumed, the authorities of the day were left to piece together who the traveler was and how he came to rest in the woods behind the stagecoach stop. After close examination of the remains and a conscious mind as to the activities of the tavern folk, the conclusion was drawn that this unknown man was indeed murdered near the tavern and buried in the back woods. Furthermore, the authorities were able to conclude that the crime was, more than likely, the result of a robbery gone awry. The identity of the traveler, however, still eluded them. Though the medical examination techniques of the day were rudimentary at best, one noteworthy characteristic of the traveler's remains enabled the pieces of the mystery to fall into place.

In 1832, Abraham Snyder, his wife Veronica and sons Michael and baby Jacob lived in a log cabin near the corner of Main Street and Harlem Road. Abraham Snyder was, like many early frontiersmen, an entrepreneur. He wanted to take the forest-clad regions of Western New York and build upon them. Though his exact plans are unknown, it is certain that he was interested in purchasing a great deal of land in the Harris Hill region of Clarence. While the Snyders saved their earnings, Abraham was able to work out a deal with the owners of the land; for several hundred dollars, the property would be his. After a bit of hard work and successful farming, Abraham and his family were soon able to gather the necessary sum. Finally, with his dreams in one pocket and the cash in the other, Abraham boarded an eastbound stagecoach to complete his transaction. Although his beneficiaries waited, Abraham never arrived at Harris Hill. Tragically, Abraham never returned home either.

For many years, the Snyder family received no word about the whereabouts of Abraham Snyder. Knowing that Abraham was not the sort of man to run out on his family, it was commonly assumed that something had happened to him between the time he boarded the stagecoach near his home and the time he was supposed to arrive in Harris Hill. For this reason, when the traveler was exhumed behind the stagecoach stop, speculation grew that the remains were those of Abraham Snyder. Speculation, however, was the extent of it. Apparently, there was not one person who claimed to recollect the crime or offer any pertinent information regarding the answer to the mystery. Therefore, the only tangible evidence authorities had to work with was the grave and the skeleton itself. The grave site, unfortunately, lacked any traces of personal belongings or other clues to the mystery. As for the remains, the doctors of that day could not, for example, compare dental records to identify the body. It was at this point that the people who had known Abraham Snyder provided a key bit of information: Abraham had a very oddly shaped skull. By glancing at a tintype taken of Abraham on his wedding day, his great-great-granddaughter, Beulah Snyder Fiddler, was able to conclude that the term "oddly shaped" must be in reference to his profile. In the photograph, it would appear as if Abraham Snyder's forehead was much shorter than the back of his head. Looking at him from the side, therefore, his head appears to come to a point. Regardless of the particulars, someone must not have been entirely persuaded by this skull-based identification. A close look at the Snyder memorial plot in the Williamsville Cemetery shows that Abraham Snyder is conspicuously left out. Though many generations of Snyders are buried within one hundred feet of each other, Abraham was never included. Whatever the reason, Abraham Snyder rests alone in a location unknown to all of his remaining offspring.

Although seemingly devastating for both boys, Abraham's murder would affect the children in very different ways. For baby Jacob, this event robbed him of his chance to know his father and grow up in a household with two loving parents. For twelve-year-old Michael, the event was inherently more complex. Though his loss of a parent was tragic, Michael now found himself "the man of the house" and in need of a way to provide for his mother and baby brother. Stricken of both his father and his childhood, Michael Snyder was able to turn disaster into strength. No one could have predicted the impact that Michael's lifetime would have on the Amherst wilderness, the growing community of Snyder and the six generations of Snyder residents to come.

The Mercantile and Snyder's Inn

In the five years following the disappearance of his father, a teenaged Michael Snyder did his best to support his mother and care for his younger brother. By the time he was seventeen, Michael had moved his family into a white plank house on the northeast corner of Main Street and Harlem Road. This house is fondly remembered by many as having spacious rooms with high ceilings, long and winding hallways and an abundance of beautifully crafted woodwork. Michael wanted nothing but the best for his mother and brother. Positioned on a three-acre plot, the Snyders' house and property extended north down Harlem Road through the lots currently occupied by Manhattan Bagel and Snyder Square North. Whether he knew it at the time, the birth of this Snyder estate would directly affect the birth of the region that would bear his name. Hence, in the later part of the 1830s, Michael Snyder took the first step toward immortality.

In the late 1830s and early 1840s, the world marveled at the development of the steel plow, the wonders of anesthesia and the efficacy of the telegraph. Stephen Foster sang "Camptown Races" and Edgar Allan Poe disturbed the world with his visions. Soon, as Longfellow and Emerson charmed readers with their insights, Charles Goodyear stunned the nation with his recipe for rubber. Finally, as Oberlin College became the first in the nation to open its doors to women, Michael Snyder prepared to open a pivotal door of his own.

And so it was in 1837 that Michael Snyder took his maiden plunge into business. Using the front room of his plank house, Michael and John Schenck, his wife's cousin, opened a mercantile. Traveling to Buffalo once a week to replenish their supplies, the men offered the residents of the area their first chance at convenient shopping. As the first genuine business to operate out of the immediate Snyder area, this opening marks the true beginning of the village that became Snyderville.

As luck would have it, Michael's granddaughter, and my grandmother, Beulah Snyder Fiddler (1895–1957), began recording her memories of Snyderville in the decades prior to her death. In her diaries, she recounts her adventures of growing up in Snyderville, as well as the many stories told to her by her grandfather. It was in these pages that she recounted the following memory of the mercantile:

> *It was a typical country store with the proverbial cracker-barrel and molasses barrel.* [The mercantile's] *central heating was provided by the pot-bellied wood stove located in the middle of the store. It was around this stove that the men gathered on winter days to exchange gossip and jokes.* [As a result of this], *the mercantile became the political center of the tiny village and it was here that matters of grave concern to the village were discussed.*

It seems, therefore, that the mercantile's effect on the area was twofold. It not only provided a close place to purchase necessities but also a location for the pioneers to gather and form the bonds needed to create a true community. Although still without a name, a village had been born between Buffalo and Williamsville, and it was only a matter of time before this village attracted some of the best and brightest personalities this young country had to offer.

Wishing to capitalize on this success, Michael began construction of his next venture. Extending the front of the Snyder house toward Main Street, Michael created a new room and a new business. Connecting it to the mercantile, Michael opened a tavern and christened it Snyder's Inn. He also constructed a second-floor ballroom for more formal occasions. With these additions, he believed that the people of the community could gather more comfortably and socialize with friends and family. Eventually, however, the clientele of the tavern hailed from far beyond the tiny community. My grandmother Beulah spoke of a diverse sampling of pioneers who frequented the tavern that was conveniently located along the Buffalo Road.

MICHAEL SNYDER HOMESTEAD. SNYDER. N.Y. 26

Michael Snyder's homestead at the northeast corner of Main Street and Harlem Road also served as the mercantile and Snyder's Inn.

The first to discover Snyder's Inn were the wayfarers. Apparently, travelers from as near as Williamsville or as far as Canandaigua would frequently make a last stop at the tavern before completing their final shuffle off to Buffalo. As the customers left, they carried with them the message of the good service and good Snyder people along the trail. In time, Michael's fame grew as both a businessman and humanitarian. Eventually, alongside the townsfolk and wayfarers, hobos who traveled the Buffalo Road would also drop by Snyder's Inn. Now a widely recognized friend to all people, Michael allowed the hobos to trade various services in return for food and rest. With regard to this open-door policy, Michael had only one rule: he asked the hobos to relinquish all matches before they retired to his back barn for the night. Without fail, Michael returned all matches to the men in the morning. Finally, in a time when the white man's treatment of Native Americans was frequently unspeakable, the Snyders also opened their doors and their hearts to the people of the Seneca Indian Nation.

At this time in history, a large Seneca Indian population resided in the vicinity of present-day South Buffalo. Conducting affairs in various parts of the region, many Native Americans would also frequent Snyder's Inn for food and rest. Recognizing that his Seneca clients did not carry American currency, Michael decided to accept articles of their handiwork as payment. The Snyders' hospitality and barter system was rapidly acknowledged by the Senecas and the inn soon gained notoriety as a favorite of the Seneca people. Unfortunately, Indians' visits to the inn were not always under the best of circumstances. One incident in particular remains an unmistakable piece of family legend. As a matter of fact, Michael's brother Jacob spoke of this event in a *Buffalo Sunday Times* article on September 19, 1924, and the heart-shaped piece of beaded leather in his hand proved it to be more than mere legend.

On what most likely began as a typical day for Michael, his mother and Jacob, their routine affairs were suddenly interrupted by a visit from a desperate stranger. With two papooses on her back, a Native American woman wearily arrived at Snyder's Inn. The family quickly noticed that the woman was covered with bruises and seemed in a great deal of peril. Unabashedly welcoming her in, the family attempted to console the stranger and attend to her ailments. At the Snyders' prompting, the woman confessed that she had married a man who was cruel and frequently abused her. In a desperate attempt to save her life, the woman had fled the reservation after a particularly violent confrontation. She admitted to being unsure of her destination but vowed never to return home. Recognizing that the woman was in no physical condition to continue fleeing, the family took her into their home and cared for her. Feeling both grateful and indebted to Michael Snyder, the woman decided to give him something very special. As a symbol of her appreciation, she placed a heart-shaped piece of leather material in his hand. The leather had been craftily designed and beaded in typical Seneca fashion. As she gave it to him she explained that this particular piece was known as the Sacred Heart of Jesus and that this piece was of great sentimental value to her. Although the Snyders doctored and fed her, the woman soon died from her extensive injuries. As Jacob later expressed in his interview, in the end, all that was left of her was the Sacred Heart of Jesus.

A century and a half after its occurrence, one is left to sit back and marvel at the hospitality and kindness that the Snyders demonstrated toward all people. Whether it was the faces they served every day or faces they encountered once in a lifetime, the Snyders greeted all faces the same. For this, they should be remembered fondly.

SNYDER'S RUG SHOP AND VINEGAR WORKS

Even with the mercantile and Snyder's Inn doing well, Michael had not yet satisfied his desire to improve upon the growing township. Being a man of many talents, Michael set forth to accommodate all of his interests and make them available to the general community. With interests ranging from politics to music, the completion of his dream was no easy task. Over the next half a century, Michael initiated at least seven more buildings in the immediate vicinity, each adding to the financial as well as cultural richness of this tiny hamlet.

Beginning our account at the Snyder homestead, Michael utilized the back acreage to house several subsidiary buildings, each containing his most recent endeavors. Directly behind the Snyder house, Michael erected a small shop where he wove rugs and carpets. Finding the act both pleasurable and profitable, Michael not only adorned the house and inn with his creations, but also offered them for sale in the mercantile. When not weaving rugs, Michael could be found in a barn farther north on the property. It is from this location that Michael operated Snyder's cider mill, eventually designated the Vinegar Works. Though this was initially a hand-operated mill, as technology and opportunity grew, Michael saw fit to convert the operation to a power facility. The power, in this case, was supplied by a single horse walking in a circle.

In her notes on Snyderville, Beulah Snyder Fiddler reminisced about this cider mill with an amusing story. She explained how Michael was always fond of the children of the community and allowed them to run on his property and play hide-and-seek in his buildings. The boys particularly enjoyed playing climbing games and swinging from "dangerous" heights. Beulah tells a famous family tale about the unlucky fate of one such adventurous, albeit uncoordinated, youth. Apparently one afternoon the boys were scaling the walls of the Vinegar Works and hanging from the building's high crossbeams. Although most of the boys in attendance were experienced climbers, there was one eager young child who was new to the sport. Boys being boys, they tempted this inexperienced athlete to climb to the highest beam and hang over the cider pit. In what I can assume was a desperate attempt to both fit into the crowd and prove worthy of his increasing testosterone levels, the boy confidently ascended the beams in the barn. Triumphantly, the boy reached the crossbeam and hung over the cider pit with the glory of a thousand men. Although Andy Warhol said that everyone has their fifteen minutes of fame, this boy enjoyed about fifteen seconds before he and his ego plunged feet first into the cider pit below. The pit, being of considerable size, was virtually impossible to escape from. As the boy treaded cider, his tempters ran to alert Mr. Snyder of the calamity. Within minutes, the men of the town gathered in the Vinegar Works and extended ropes to the fallen hero. With a long face and half of the town in attendance, the boy was eventually hoisted out of the pit. Except for being a little sticky and positively humiliated, the boy was returned to his parents without injury.

THE BLACKSMITH SHOP AND WAGON WORKS OF SNYDER

In 1860, Michael began to extend his holdings to property located eastward on Main Street. In the basic vicinity of our present Snyder Square East and Siena Restaurant, Michael erected two buildings with the sole intention of renting them to appropriate craftsmen. In an effort to bring some desperately needed services to the growing village, Michael constructed Snyder's first wagon shop and blacksmith shop. With the addition of these craftsmen, the village was on its way to becoming self-sufficient and gaining complete independence from Williamsville's and Buffalo's "technology." By 1900, George Helfter had established himself in both buildings and created Helfter's Wagon Works and Helfter's Iron Works. As the sole tenant

Helfter's Wagon Works and Blacksmith Shop was located on the north side of Main Street between Harlem Road and Freuhauf Drive.

of these buildings, he also participated in Michael's unique "rent to own" plan for each structure. Having not built these businesses as a profit-making endeavor, Michael was more than pleased to allow the Helfters to pay rent for each business and have it applied toward the total sale price. Already a successful businessman, Michael was more interested in having another family establish itself as profitable tenants of Snyderville than in his own gains from the income property. Although Michael saw his generosity as a way to promote the village, it is ironic that these very buildings would ultimately result in the town's demise. At this pleasant time in Snyder's history, no one could have been aware of the tragic role Helfter's buildings would play in the devastating fire of 1905.

SNYDER'S BAND HALL

Although Michael dabbled in several businesses and services, none gained more publicity than Snyder's band hall. Also used as a recreation center, Michael completed a small plank building on the northeast side of Main Street and Harlem Road. Presently occupied by Snyder Square, the band hall was located in almost the exact location of the popular Café in the Square. In this venture, Michael became a formidable version of Meredith Wilson's *Music Man*. Acting as Snyder's own "Harold Hill," Michael offered music lessons to the children of the village and sold instruments on the "installment plan." For Michael, the installment plan meant that the families paid him whenever they could; frequently, Michael never collected a cent. For the village's enjoyment, concerts were usually sponsored at the band hall on Monday and Thursday evenings. Performers ranged from talented townsfolk to more well-known musical acts. The lighting for the event was always provided by an array of candles. Most of these candles were mounted in candle holders that adorned the perimeter of the room. Being pieces of artwork all unto themselves, a few of these candle holders were donated to the Snyder collection at the Amherst Museum.

At that time, to have a band hall of this nature was a very prestigious accomplishment. As is the custom today, events that were thought to be culturally enriching were frequently covered by the local press. On May 1, 1879, a reporter from the *Amherst Bee* attended one such event and wrote of it in the "Social Notes" section of the next edition. As luck would have it, the press found this evening to be a truly noteworthy event. The article begins on a traditional note, stating, "A social party was enjoyed at Mr. M.

Snyder's Hall last Wednesday night by the young people. Folgelsonger's Band furnished the music…assisted by several members of the Eggertsville Concert Band." The article continues, reporting how the affair was "kept up until an early hour," and nearing the end of the night "one of the members of the band moved his chair back a little too far on the stage and by doing so, had the misfortune of falling backward, taking the drop curtain with him. He picked himself up as quick as he could and played his part as though nothing had happened." Despite this minor accident, the paper reported that "the drop curtain was replaced in a few minutes and all were again tripping the light fantastic."

The drop curtain spoken of in this article, incidentally, has a rather interesting history of its own. If you recall, Michael Snyder frequently allowed hobos to sleep in his barn and eat in Snyder's Inn. As payment for this generosity, Michael would accept a small amount of goods or services. On one occasion, the Snyders were fortunate enough to open their doors to a gentleman with a very special talent. Although he had no money, the stranger agreed to make a trade with Michael for food and shelter. Upon agreement, the man immediately set to his important task—painting a curtain for use in Snyder's band hall. Once completed, this exquisite curtain presided over many an event in the busy hall. It was this curtain that broke the fall of one clumsy, but lucky, musician.

THE SNYDERVILLE POST OFFICE

After all of the businesses established, buildings erected and positions filled by Michael Snyder, the decision to name the village in his honor was not made until after the construction of his next venture. Choosing a plot across from his homestead, Michael erected Snyder's first post office on the northwest corner of Main Street and Harlem Road. Using the front of the building to relocate his general store, Michael set up an official United States Post Office in the rear. The date of this opening, however, is the cause of a great deal of debate. Snyder family records indicate the existence of the post office as far back as the 1840s. It is also a common family story that the day President Lincoln was assassinated, Michael lowered the American flag from the front of the post office and preserved it in tribute and memorial to the fallen president. Following this, the post office is listed in a published *Snyder's Business Directory* from 1866. It is most perplexing, therefore, when one consults the official United States Post Office records and finds that Michael Snyder was

Postmaster Michael Snyder stands by the original Snyderville Post Office, in the hamlet named in his honor.

not officially recognized as postmaster of the Snyderville Post Office until 1882. Furthermore, the *Amherst Bee* reported on August 10, 1882, "During the past week, a post office has been established at Snyderville, to be called Snyder, with Michael Snyder as postmaster." Although providing little help with regard to the date of the post office's inception, this tidbit from the paper alludes to this instance as the prompt for when the "ville" was officially dropped from the Snyderville moniker.

Regardless of the exact date of inception, Michael Snyder was the first to expose Snyder to the widespread wonders of the United States mail. Serving as postmaster with the same sort of tenacity and longevity with which he served his other endeavors, Michael remained the village's postmaster for forty years. When Michael finally retired, he turned the daily running of the post office over to Jacob C. Freuhauf, for whom Freuhauf Drive is named. After a relatively brief reign, Freuhauf was succeeded by Michael's son, Tobias Snyder, in 1890. In his father's image, "Tobe" accumulated twenty-two years of postal service before his own retirement

The original Snyderville Post Office was eventually moved to the rear of the Harlem Road and Main Street corner and converted to a home.

in 1912. Following Tobe's departure, the Snyderville Post Office was headed by a handful of Snyder residents over the next eighteen years. In 1930, the original Snyderville Post Office was disbanded.

SNYDER'S COURTHOUSE

Shifting from entertainment to politics, Michael also found himself engulfed in the political hierarchy of his time. Having established himself as a prominent citizen of both Snyderville and Amherst at large, Michael soon saw fit to venture into the political arena. Wishing to occupy another vacancy in Snyder Village, Michael quickly promoted himself as Snyder's first justice of the peace. Not seeing the need to build a formal courthouse, Michael constructed a court on the second floor of his home. So as not to disturb the residence and business of downstairs, Michael added an outside stairway for easier access to the room. Once inside, the legal needs of this relatively small village centered on collecting fines, signing legal papers and performing marriages. Finding himself both well received by the village and interested in his work, Michael Snyder continued to serve as Snyder's justice of the peace for the next forty-two years.

As part of his "official" duties, Michael would act as auctioneer for the village whenever the need arose. Being both a prestigious position and a formidable skill, Michael took his auction work very seriously. Whether involving livestock, landholdings or personal property, Michael was able to motivate a crowd and inspire top-dollar prices for all goods involved. Notoriety of Michael's "fast-talking" talent grew and eventually extended outside of Snyder's boundaries. Making him an offer he could not refuse, the town of Amherst soon had its first Snyder resident in the role of "Official Auctioneer of the Town of Amherst." In years following, Michael's son Abraham would follow in his father's footsteps and also lend his talents to the auction arena.

CHAPTER THREE

TRANSPORTATION

Stagecoaches, Trolleys and Tollgates

W anting the interests of his growing village well represented in all business conducted by the town of Amherst, Michael Snyder also held several town offices and provided various key functions for his extended community. Most impressively, in 1871 Michael was elected to the esteemed office of "Supervisor of the Town of Amherst." After serving a one-year term, however, Michael saw fit to switch his efforts to a less demanding position: "Amherst Highway Commissioner." Although many may find this title laughable when comparing the "highways" of Michael's time to the highways of today, there were many unique conditions that had to be accounted for. In Beulah Snyder Fiddler's notes, for instance, she mentions how the Buffalo Road was virtually inoperable in the dry weather because the dust kicked up by the horses was "almost unbearable." It seems, therefore, that instead of filling potholes, the nineteenth-century highway commissioners may have been concerned with dust reduction.

EARLY ROADS AND THE MAIN STREET TOLLGATE

The records of this time allude to only a few operable roads in the immediate area. Standing in the heart of Snyderville, Harlem Road existed as the only true road in Snyderville that ran north–south. According to Snyder family notes, the early Harlem Road extended from a "point below the hill" on the north side to the Kensington Avenue area on the south. At this time it is believed that Harlem Road hill extended far beyond the present-day Park School and ended in the vicinity of Sheridan Drive. This, in fact, may be how Sheridan Drive came to rest at its present location. On the south end of Harlem Road, a small stretch of Kensington Avenue was also in existence. The poor condition of the road, however, left it considered only a pathway and not fit for serious travel.

To the west of Snyderville, there existed two frequently traveled roads. Named in honor of Eggertsville's first postmaster, Joseph Eggert, Eggert Road ran in a north–south direction near its present location. Though records are scarce, it is believed that Eggert Road extended almost all the way to Kensington Avenue on the south. The exact length of the north side, however, is unclear. Running somewhat parallel to Eggert Road, Springville Avenue was also operable. Although only about half as long as its current span, Springville Avenue was frequently traveled by the pioneers of the day.

As mentioned earlier, the only official road traveling to and from Buffalo was the dirt road called the Great Trail or Buffalo Road (presently Main Street). Depending on the season, unfortunately, travel on this road could be made unpleasant by various weather conditions. In the dry weather, the dust would swarm around the horses' feet, and in the rainy season, the mud could get deep enough to trap a wagon. There were also small stretches of road that had been filled with crushed stone from a quarry on Main Street. Though this may have given temporary relief from the dust and mud, it was not without consequence. When a horse or wagon traveled the road, the stone would be ground into a fine white powder. As the traffic passed, a film of ground stone would settle like snowfall on everything around. This, as one can imagine, could get quite irritating.

In addition to these few roads, as highway commissioner, Michael Snyder was in charge of one other key element of the "highways." Established in 1839, a tiny plank building known as the Main Street Tollgate stood watch over the local traffic for generations. Located about three hundred feet west of the corner of Main Street and Getzville Road, the tollgate building stood a short distance west of where Daemen College now resides. The inside of the structure was modest but comfortable, and it came complete with adjacent living quarters for the gatekeeper. The outside of the building had a covered passage for vehicles or animals and a platform on each side of the gate was covered with planking. It was the sound of traffic on this planking that alerted the gatekeeper that business was approaching. For the first forty-four years, this position was occupied by various members of the Oberholser family. As documented in an *Amherst Bee* article from October 18, 1883:

The [Main Street] *toll-gate, which for the past forty-four years has been in the keeping of Mr. John Oberholser and family, has, since the death of this old gentleman, passed into the care of Miss Hattie Magoffin. Miss Nancy Oberholser is at present with her sister Mrs. Watson, and Miss Leah Oberholser has made her home with Mrs. John Gotwalt of this village, also a sister. The pleasant and familiar face of Miss Leah will be missed by hundreds of travelers who have had occasion to use the gate in the past years.*

Succeeding Hattie Magoffin as gatekeeper were Grey Lee, Elijah and Jacob Long, Benjamin and Mary Fry and finally their sons Charles and Frank Fry. It is said that beyond the obvious duties of these gatekeepers, they also provided key services such as disseminating news brought by travelers and carrying important messages to village leaders. Sometimes, the gatekeepers were even witness to some newsworthy events. As reported by the *Amherst Bee* on December 14, 1882:

Last Friday evening as John Ernst of Amherst and Wm. Smith of Lancaster were returning from a party at Buffalo Plains, they stopped at Mr. A. Krumholtz. While in his place a train came along, frightening the horse, causing the animal to break the strap and run away. He was brought up at the toll gate, where he got tangled in the blanket and was caught. The seat and an accordion belonging to Mr. Ernst were badly damaged.

In dealing with business matters, the gatekeepers were often expected to employ their better judgment when encountering "cash poor" farmers. Reportedly, it was common practice to defer the tolls for farmers on their way to Buffalo's Chippewa Market. After successfully dealing their goods and livestock, the grateful citizens would pay their balance on the way back home.

Operating as one would assume, the Main Street Tollgate was an official governance with town-designated prices. In what seemed an outrageous fee to small farmers, it was agreed during the Fry brothers' tenure that all travelers would be charged two cents for a single wagon and horse going as far as Getzville Road, four cents to proceed to Fogelsonger Road (now Park Club Lane) and five cents to continue to Williamsville. For teams, the price rose to four, six and eight cents respectively. Just as all present-day drivers learn alternate routes to avoid the toll roads, so too did early residents of Amherst create alternate routes to Buffalo. Nicknamed "the Shunpike," farmers would

The Main Street Tollgate stood on Main Street a few hundred yards west of Getzville Road. The gatekeepers resided in the adjacent gatehouse.

commonly avoid the Main Street Tollgate by driving Kensington Avenue far enough west to bypass the station. To accomplish this, the culprits would be forced to use Eggert Road or old farmers' paths to make the cut back up to Main Street. The conditions of these unofficial paths, however, were frequently degenerative, and the landowners were less than delighted by the unwelcome traffic.

In another effort to avoid paying the toll, some travelers would attempt to speed through the gate before the gatekeeper emerged. These attempts, however, were usually ill planned, considering most faces were familiar in a town of this size. Invariably, the gatekeeper would be able to catch a glimpse of the driver or could sometimes recognize the outlaw simply from his horse or rig. Charles Fry, one of the last gatekeepers, reminisced about several similar situations. In one such situation, it is told that Charles was sitting in the living quarters as he heard a wagon approaching from the westbound direction. As he glanced out the window, he saw a figure returning from Buffalo with a horse-drawn wagon. Before Charles could emerge from the building, the perpetrator whipped the horses into a fury. Chaotically clamoring across the wooden planking, the rig sped haphazardly through the gate. Not willing to let his perpetrator get the best of him, Charles jumped on a horse of his own and rode wildly toward Williamsville. Utilizing shortcuts available only to a single horse, Charles was able to reach the village before the wagon. When the perpetrator arrived in Williamsville, he was unwittingly greeted by a disheartening surprise. Having secured both his self-respect and a warrant for the man's arrest, Charles Fry confronted his criminal with great satisfaction. Being more interested in his victory than the man's incarceration, however, Charles agreed to accept the eight cents for the toll and release his prisoner. Another case was reported in a newspaper interview of Charles Fry from April 6, 1953. In it, Fry recalls the events surrounding "an attempt by an intoxicated man to 'run the gate' without paying the toll. Fry, who held the two mile running championship at Colgate with the then amazing time of 10:19, took off after the team, passed it and was waiting in Buffalo with a warrant when the team came trotting along the road. The farmer admitted his guilt and was fined $10."

After restructuring its Highway Department in 1899, the town of Amherst elected to disband the Main Street Tollgate. On October 13, 1899, the tollgate and gatekeeper's house were put up for public auction. Although there is no official record, it is probable that Michael Snyder was still in service as town auctioneer at this time. Regardless of whether it was Michael's or another voice that called out the bids, the Main Street Tollgate was eventually bought by Edward Wingert and Eugene P. Ouchie for the incredible sum of $29.50.

MEANS OF PUBLIC TRANSPORTATION

In an effort to avoid the unpleasantness of the road conditions, townsfolk frequently sought public transportation when venturing to the city. The earliest means of public transport was an unnamed covered wagon drawn by four horses. The schedule for excursions was erratic and the wagon was bumpy, but the trip was usually made successfully. Eventually, a handsome stagecoach entered the area to succeed the covered wagon. Downsized to a mere two horses, the "Black Meriah" routinely made one trip to Buffalo

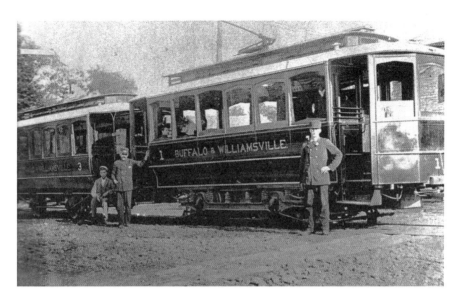

The Toonerville Trolley ran down the north side of Main Street from 1893 to 1930, providing citizens with quick and consistent travel from Williamsville to Buffalo.

each day and returned on schedule each night. With the addition of glass windows, the people found this stagecoach quite appealing. A successful venture, the Black Meriah remained in operation until 1893, when trolley service to Buffalo was established. Over a century after its demise, however, a reminder of the old stage is still evident to people who travel the intersection of Washington and Kings Highways. While a novice observer may notice that the intersection is unusually large and a bit misshapen, the informed will recognize that this section was a turnaround for the daily stage. Located a comfortable distance from Main Street, this intersection was used to turn the horses and afford the drivers a chance to rest between runs.

In 1892, construction began for the new Buffalo and Williamsville Electronic Railway. Working along the north side of Main Street, crews began the process of installing tracks from the village of Williamsville through Snyder and Eggertsville and ending at the city line. To begin the project, steam engines were employed to plow up the surface of Main Street and men were employed to rake and level the trolley's pathway. Following this, stone was harvested from Fogelsonger's quarry and used to lay the firm foundation, on which 4.5 miles of trolley track was laid.

On April 5, 1893, the excited citizens of Snyder joined their Williamsville and Eggertsville neighbors on Main Street at Buffalo's city line. In parade-like fashion, old and young formed a large procession and followed the entire arsenal of the railway, four total cars, in its inaugural voyage down the trolley tracks. Once in full operation, the "Toonerville Trolley," as the people affectionately called it, ran to and from the city several times a day. Although departures were originally scheduled on an hourly basis, popularity soon shortened this wait to thirty minutes and eventually to an aggressive twelve-minute schedule. In its heyday, it is estimated that over four hundred residents rode the trolley every day. After purchasing a ticket, riders could choose between two closed cars and two open cars. The closed cars were heated by stoves in the winter and the open cars boasted curtains to shield them from the rain. The front of the trolley even had a plow hookup for the nasty winter months. Operations were coordinated out of a small depot at the city line, complete with a waiting room and small store. In the official records, it is listed that the trolley made stops at Eggert Road, Ivyhurst and Harlem Road, before continuing to Williamsville. When Snyder family descendant Viola Hunt was naïvely asked about the railway stops, a little perplexed, she simply described how the conductor would pick her up and drop her off in front of her Main Street house. Nevertheless, with the inception of this railway, travel to and from the city became easy. What was once a half-day trip could now be accomplished in under an hour. For the Buffalo businessmen in

The Toonerville Trolley tracks run in front of the Snyder Post Office building on the north side of Main Street near Harlem Road.

particular, this convenience gave them freedoms that they had not previously enjoyed. Most importantly, the Toonerville Trolley afforded them their first opportunity to leave the city and relocate into something called "a suburb."

Discussing the trolley with those who remember it is always an opportunity for enjoyment. Everyone seems to have their favorite memories of this fabled time and they can range from the sentimental to the bizarre. For example, it seems as if the pranksters of the community would use this trolley as a surefire chance for mischief. More than one of Snyder's elder gentlemen has described a prank involving the disconnection of the trolley's electricity. Apparently, the corner of Main Street and Chateau Terrace was a prime venue for this due to the location of the electricity cable. An early Chateau resident laughed as he recalled waiting to hear the trolley approaching and then sprinting the three hundred yards to the corner to disconnect the cable. Having already scouted perfect hiding spots, the children would watch in enjoyment as the befuddled conductor would jump off the car and run to reconnect the cable.

Being reared in the "bus stop generation," it is hard not to find this free-spirited trolley incredibly romantic. Living through the memories of others, it is easy to picture their Snyderville as a scene from *Meet Me in St. Louis*, with Judy Garland and Margaret O'Brien singing "clang clang clang goes the trolley…" Regardless of the community's love of the railway, however, the Toonerville Trolley was slated to be removed in September 1930 when the Buffalo Transit Company announced the establishment of a bus service. With the same sort of fanfare with which it was ordained, the people of the community celebrated the retirement of the railway in an epic way. Draping the oldest car in black cloth and perching it on the back of a truck, the community proceeded with a "funeral procession" for their beloved trolley, proudly escorting it to Buffalo City Hall. Thus, with their new transportation system in effect, the people of Snyder officially traded the quaintness of the carefree trolley for the ease and predictability of a metro bus schedule.

CHAPTER FOUR

THE SNYDER FAMILY

A Look through the Generations

As previously stated, Abraham and Veronica Snyder were fortunate enough to have two healthy boys to carry on the Snyder name. While Michael, the oldest brother, was bound for fame and fortune, Jacob was content to frolic in Michael's shadow. It seems apparent that, although Michael seemed to have inherited enough ambition for both of them, "Jake" was certainly blessed with more than his share of personality. Content with his place as "Michael's brother," Jacob would always remain faithful to his brother's ideals. Although both boys would eventually marry and have families of their own, the lifelong bond between them was always as evident as their differences.

MICHAEL AND HIS FAMILY

An established citizen, businessman and profitable entrepreneur for well over a decade, Michael Snyder eventually fell victim to the charms of a different sort of entrepreneur. Her name was Catherine, and she wanted to build a life for Michael. Hence, in 1851, thirty-two-year old Michael Snyder married Catherine Halter, a Buffalo native. One decade his junior, Catherine was born on June 22, 1830, and remained in the Buffalo area her entire life. Already considered "old" at the time of his marriage, Michael and Catherine wasted no time in starting their family. With their first child born that same year, the Snyders would give life to a total of eleven children in a period spanning twenty-three years.

Forever a patriot, Michael Snyder made a point to name each of his six sons after famous American men. First came Henry Franklin (1851–1869), Edward Daniel (1858–1939) and Tobias Washington (1860–1941). Voicing their support during the Civil War, the Snyders next welcomed Abraham Lincoln (1863–1934). Following the war, Solomon Sherman (1866–1934) and his brother Charles Grant (1868–1953) rounded out the male side of the family. The Snyder daughters, on the contrary, were able to escape the famous name plight. Five in number, the Snyder daughters were Mary Elizabeth (1853–1936), Elma Amanda (1856–1934), Susan (1863–1863), Ida Elvira (1871–1876) and Alta Melvina (1874–1948). It is interesting to note that while the Snyders had the misfortune of losing one child at birth and others at ages five and seventeen, the remaining eight children all lived well into old age.

Socially as well as politically, the Snyders played an important role in the tiny hamlet. One tradition, long since spoken of, involved the custom of the "Hunt and Feast." Apparently, on such a designated day, a group of hunters from the hamlet would gather together early in the morning for a day of essential as well as recreational hunting. At this time, remember, forests still covered much of the nearby land and served as a prosperous venue for both food and sport. According to the tradition, as the men spent the daylight searching for dinner, Catherine Snyder spent it making preparations for the upcoming feast. I am told that in honor of this happy event, Catherine would even adorn her twenty-foot dining table with all the finest trimmings. When the hunters returned, Catherine would unquestioningly offer her hospitality to both the fortuitous and the disgruntled. All involved in the ritual would then spend the evening feasting and laughing with their good food and good friends. There was, however, one reported "catch" to this tradition. Apparently, as part of the custom, it was always agreed that the hunter showing the *least* evidence of a successful day would have to pay for all the dinners. Apparently this was the generation of irony.

JACOB AND HIS FAMILY

Eventually, Jacob Snyder also surrendered to the enchanting sound of wedding bells. Moving from one influential family to another, Jacob Snyder married Fanny Long (1832–1907) of the Williamsville Longs. The Long family came to Amherst in 1808 from an undisclosed region of Canada and soon became large landowners. By 1819, Abraham Long had been named commissioner of highways and served as a part-time justice of the peace. In his passing, the Long family lent its name to North and South Long Streets in Williamsville, lent its property to the Williamsville Cemetery and continued to be an intricate part of this region for many generations to come.

In any event, by choosing Fanny Long for his wife, Jacob Snyder was able to become a part of a family as deeply rooted and successful as his own. Together, Jake and Fanny gave birth to two children, John (birth date unknown) and Benjamin (1855–1923). Once grown, Benjamin Snyder also married into a family who was familiar to the hamlet. Having grown up in such close vicinity, Benjamin Snyder soon met and married Susanna Fogelsonger (1848–1929). The Fogelsonger family owned the quarry on Main Street and had a band that frequently played at Snyder's band hall.

Even though most of his life was spent out of the limelight, over half a century after his death, Jake's love for his wife was on display at the Amherst Museum. In the middle 1990s, a few treasured mementos from Jake and Fanny's happy marriage were on display inside a modestly arranged display case. Of these tiny trinkets was a dainty gold pocket watch that Jake reportedly gave to Fanny on their golden wedding anniversary. The watch wasn't extravagant or ordained with an abundance of gaudy jewels. The tiny timepiece appeared reliable in its mechanics and pure in its simplicity—the way one imagines their love to have been.

With regard to personality, Jake Snyder was, by all accounts, a most peculiar fellow. Known for his quick wit and subtle quirkiness, Jake Snyder could always be counted on for a good time. The most convincing evidence for this lies within his *Buffalo Sunday Times* interview printed September 14, 1924. This article boasts the headline "Jake Snyder and Old Homestead are Reminders of Pioneer Days" and prominently displays a five- by seven-inch photograph of Jake posing in front of a ferryboat backdrop. Seated on what seems to be a large contraption of cleverly tied branches and logs, a white-haired Jake Snyder grimaces at the camera with all the rugged stiffness of that ridiculous chair. Looking remarkably like Mark Twain in a heavy black suit, this black-and-white picture of Jake sets the stage for a wildly colorful dissertation of a man and his version of the past.

As far as the article itself, the author soon buries himself under a cavalcade of misinterpretations and backward facts. Even the caption to the picture is untrue. Whether these discrepancies are due to the rumblings of a ninety-three-year-old man or the overzealous generalization of a green reporter, however, will never be determined. Right from the onset, the reader is misled by a subtitle that reads "He Founded Local Suburb Snyder" and

Ninety-three-year-old Jacob Snyder as he appeared in a 1924 *Buffalo Sunday Times* article.

the accompanying picture captioned, "Jacob Snyder, who founded suburb Snyderville." Obviously, anyone privy to the timeline of events would agree that founding Snyder would be quite a feat for a baby who wasn't even born until nine years after the Snyders' arrived. To the article's credit, it did mention that Jacob had a brother, but continues to clearly name Jacob as the father of Snyderville. Oddly enough, it also names Jacob as the father of Michael's children.

Despite these colorful riddles, the crux of this article is still fascinating. Following the problematic introduction, the article commences with commentary from an interview Jacob gave about the village of Snyder, the Snyder family, their homestead and the city of Buffalo. With all the gumption of a traveling salesman, Jake recounts events from his life, tells stories about his family and dispenses his outlook for the future. Weeding through the bombastic grammar and erratic writing style of the early 1920s, it is still evident that Jake Snyder was a born storyteller. The candor with which he speaks enables the reader to feel as if Jake were truly talking to him across a bar while chomping peanuts and spitting tobacco. In one such example, Jake tells of the following occurrence on the sidewalk of "Delaware near Mohawk": "In those days, swine and cattle were allowed to roam for forage in the streets of the city. I was walking along the street [one day] when the animal charged with fury and bowled me over. I was only saved from the fate of being reduced to sausage meat by the timely intervention of my brother Michael."

When discussing travel, Jake told of his distrust of stagecoaches and the mysterious incident involving his father, Abraham. He continued, nevertheless, to describe the following stagecoach adventure of his own: "In 1854 I went to New York City in a stagecoach drawn by four horses with a two bushel mail bag strapped on behind. We took five days to make the trip. I hardly think people of today [1924] would like to travel in that style."

Jake proceeded to discuss several other important and historic topics of his time: his friendship with Red Jacket, the Seneca Indian chief; the bugle announcing the arrival and departures of Erie Canal boats; and the American Hotel fire of 1865. He recalled when the waters of Lake Erie came as far inward as the Liberty Pole on lower Main Street and the daily running of the Black Meriah streetcar. Oddly enough, he also claims to remember the cholera scourge of 1825, the murder of John Love and subsequent hanging of the three Thayer brothers in Niagara Square. All of these events, incidentally, took place before Jake was even born.

Questionable memories aside, the most entertaining sections of this exposé are the paragraphs extolling Jacob's theories on life and the human condition. After living through most of a century, Jacob seemed able to evaluate his experience with all of the technical skills of a research chemist combined with the insight and compassion of a clinical psychologist. On the subject of long life, for example, a ninety-three-year-old Jake appeared qualified to prescribe the following: live a frugal life, keep the mind happy and contented and exercise regularly. The latter, according to Jacob, accounts for the major portion of his longevity. Even though living in the Western New York area may have made the practice difficult, Jacob Snyder prided himself on his daily walks "no matter how bad the weather." Oddly enough, the superstitious may say that Jacob Snyder "jinxed" himself with this proclamation; he died within a year of this article's publication.

Fitness, it seems, was not the only area in which Jake Snyder considered himself a guru. Apparently, Jake was able to conjure up an opinion about nearly anything as long as he had an audience to entertain. With this in mind, the article concludes with Jacob's assessment of "modern youth." Concurrent with his three-step recipe for long life, Jacob's analysis of the younger generation was equally optimistic. He believed that the youth of

One of the older houses in Snyder, this property, once owned by the Snyder brothers, is located on Harlem Road, north of Main Street.

the early 1920s were more able to take care of themselves than the children of fifty years earlier. In an effort to explain himself, Jacob Snyder concludes his interview with another fascinating observation and leaves the reader with his fondest image of crazy Jake Snyder and his buoyant outlook on life: "I have no fear for the race because of the antics of the so-called 'flappers.' They may be a little wild, but I venture to say that the average girl today is just as good as they were in my day. The boys too—although they go in for some curious fads—will probably make pretty good fathers for the coming generation."

Hence, in the words of George M. Cohan, "No time to pitch woo now, the century's new now…so be my 20th century love."

THE END OF AN ERA

Just as all that touches this earth is bound to leave it, so went the fate of Michael Snyder. After an illness that had confined him to his bed for over a month, Michael Snyder died at his homestead on December 1, 1902. The passing of Michael Snyder was the beginning of a new era for both the Snyder family and the Snyder community. While the family had lost its father and provider, the community had also lost its most important figurehead. In the wake of his absence, all who knew him were left to fill the void his departure left in their own affairs. With consideration for all that Michael had touched in his lifetime, one can only imagine that this void must have been great. For his family, in particular, the loss must have seemed immeasurable.

A very shrewd and talented businessman, Michael Snyder was fortunate enough to have accumulated a sizable fortune by the time of his death. Complete with fine possessions, extensive property and gross monetary sums, Michael's estate was entailed equally to his eight adult children. While the net worth and method of his distribution between the siblings is not clear, it is evident that all parties benefited to a substantial degree. The homestead, at the corner of Main Street and Harlem Road, remained the property of all of the unmarried Snyder children and the fortune divided between them. Without exaggeration, the money inherited by the children was enough to ensure that none of the beneficiaries would ever have to work. Most of them, incidentally, took this literally. Of those who did work, some followed in their father's footsteps and carried on positions that he had held in the community.

As the true father of Snyderville, Michael's contributions to this area were insurmountable. Most notably, Michael singlehandedly built a village complete with mercantile, band hall, wagon works, blacksmith, post office, courthouse, cider mill and Snyder's Inn. In the sixty-five years since he first ventured into business, Michael Snyder was able to hand weave a town where five generations of his offspring would grow and flourish. In the village that bore his name, Michael entertained, protected and provided for his neighbors. Although only a toddler when he arrived in Snyder, he was a legend by the time he left it. Of Michael's eighty-three years on earth, seventy-nine of them were spent in Snyder, and those seventy-nine years built our hometown.

THE SNYDER CHILDREN

The Snyder children were an odd lot. Perhaps it was growing up in the shadow of a famous father or, possibly, the sheer wealth of the family. Whatever the reason, Michael and Catherine Snyder gave birth to some of the most offbeat characters in the hamlet's history. For example, of the eight adult children, only three ever married and moved out of the homestead. The remaining five lived together in the Snyder house until the day each died. Of these five, only one ever worked.

Michael's son Tobias Washington Snyder frequently performed in Snyder's band hall.

Tobias Washington Snyder

Let us begin our discussion of the Snyder siblings with the five who lived together at the homestead. As previously told, only one of these siblings ever worked a true job; this was Tobias Snyder. You may recall from an earlier chapter that Tobe, as he was known, was the only son to succeed Michael in the postal service. Serving as Snyderville postmaster for twenty-two years, Tobias was the only one of Michael's children to capture the limelight and assume interest in his father's affairs. In addition to succeeding Michael at the post office, Tobias was also a town supervisor and weekend rug loomer. In his father's image, Tobe played in a brass band with his brothers Solomon and Edward, and the men frequently entertained at the band hall. In a sharp departure from his father, however, Tobias never married.

Charles Grant Snyder

Another bachelor, Charles Grant Snyder, never sought any kind of employment. His life bears testimony to my theory that the Snyder children were bound in scandal and peculiarity. For instance, rumor has it that, in his youth, he was a fairly untamed soul. The bulk of his time was spent at various taverns between Williamsville and Buffalo and he frequently went "missing" for days at a time. In fact, the story has been passed down that, in such an event, his siblings would make a thorough investigation of all the ditches in the area. More than once, it has been told, the Snyder siblings rescued a drunken Charlie from the Snyder roadside. Eventually, Charlie had to frequent taverns outside of the immediate area to maintain his privacy. Apparently his younger sister Alta was vividly opposed to his constant drinking and took it upon herself to become his keeper. In a scene that sounds like part of some vintage western comedy, Alta reportedly dragged her little rocking chair to the local tavern one evening. There, in front of all of Charlie's drinking buddies and treasured friends, Alta quietly rocked and stared coldly at the men. Keeping this up for quite some time, Alta's tenacity eventually paid off. Much to her delight, her vagabond brother ultimately cracked under the pressure and agreed to go home.

According to those who knew him best, Charlie occupied the rest of his free time with the wonders of horticulture. A curious fellow by nature, Charles would frequently spend his days experimenting with various horticulture mysteries. As one of his projects, Charles trained a vine of squash to climb up the side of the barn and bloom on the roof. Although this was both rewarding and entertaining in the beginning, as the years passed, the harvest

Charles Grant Snyder, one of the unmarried Snyder siblings, kept residence in the Snyder family homestead until his death.

became incrementally more difficult for the farmer. Deep into his fifties, it is reported that Charles could still be seen scaling the barn roof to monitor his crop. In his older age, however, Charles no longer felt able to make the trip. Incidentally, family legend whispers that Charlie no longer felt the need to do most things in his older age. In fact, his sisters swore that he was so lazy that he wouldn't even walk about the house anymore. Eventually, they contended, he lost the use of his legs from sheer laziness and was confined to a wheelchair. Although no one knows whether the diagnosis of Charlie's ailments was accurate, it is a fact that Charles Snyder spent the latter portion of his life wheeled about in an old wicker chair. Wouldn't it be ironic if the wealth that enabled Charlie the freedom to abstain from work eventually contributed to him losing the use of his legs? Be careful what you wish for…

Edward Daniel Snyder

In conjunction with his brother Charles, Edward Snyder also left behind traces of bizarre hobbies and embarrassing life events. Yet another Snyder sibling without gainful employment, Edward managed to keep himself busy with his various hobbies and life adventures. The most consuming of these activities, I am told, revolved around the many rituals of hunting and fishing. More interested in fishing than hunting, Ed resisted the traditional taxidermy trophies in lieu of a showcase for all of his bait and hook casualties. Although many found it particularly revolting, it seems that it was common in those days to hang fish heads in a row above the barn door. Knowing that the barn was also a special place for his brother Charles, one can only imagine the bantering that occurred every time Charles climbed over Edward's fish heads to reach his ripened squash. Apparently Charles's disgust of this practice was legendary, and mention of this was even made in the aforementioned newspaper interview by their Uncle Jake Snyder. Regardless of his family's views, however, Edward remained true to his "art" and his sport.

When he was not occupied with his animal adventures, it was assumed that Uncle Edward was living out his other unconventional "pastimes." Apparently, Uncle Edward liked to keep company with a "lady friend." Although it seems preposterous, there was, evidentially, a woman on Harlem Road with whom Edward had several children. Not only did Edward never marry the woman, but he also kept her identity, as well as those of his children, a guarded secret. All that was known in the family fold was that Edward "kept" a woman and an undisclosed number of children. With the Snyder population as small as it was, it seems extraordinary that a single woman and her children could live within a mile of the Snyders and none would ever deduce her identity. More importantly, with several unknown relatives living about in the hamlet, one has to wonder whether any of them ever accidentally intermarried. In any event, when Edward died, he left his money evenly divided between his siblings Alta, Tobe and Charlie, his nieces Agnes, Beulah and Gladys and his three adult children. His "lady friend" had apparently died before him. To further raise curiosity, even after his death, his children's identities remained a secret. The proceedings of his estate were carried out by lawyers and the identities of the three beneficiaries were never publicly disclosed. Apparently, his sister Alta was very upset about their inclusion in the will, but without knowing their identity, she could do nothing to harass them.

Mary Elizabeth Snyder

Living with the Snyder bachelors were sisters Mary and Alta Snyder. The Snyder sisters, it seems, did not escape from the peculiarity or scandal that seemed to embody their family. For example, it may be an error to refer to Mary as an unmarried sister. In her younger days, Mary Snyder was in love with a man of whom her brothers did not approve. The man was blind and her brothers did not believe that he was a suitable husband for their sister. In a desperate attempt at freedom, Mary and her suitor ran away and eloped. Upon discovering the escape, the Snyder brothers set forth to track down the couple and undo what they perceived to be a calamitous wrong. Finally locating the couple on their wedding night, the Snyder brothers denounced the marriage, stole the bride and escorted her back to the Snyder homestead. The matter was never unearthed again.

Alta Melvina Snyder

In contrast to her sister Mary, Alta Snyder was truly a spinster. Apparently she did have one boyfriend, but he died from a serious case of the measles. In retrospect, it is told that most people believed that this unfortunate ending was "lucky for him." Nevertheless, Alta reportedly kept a very large "hope chest" in the upstairs hallway that she filled with fine linens and posh household items…just in case. From most of the stories and accounts, Alta Snyder personified the notion of a busybody and was never content unless she was entangled in a scandal. At her very core, Alta was obsessed with money—hers and everyone else's. If she wasn't telling someone how to spend their money,

Alta Melvina Snyder, youngest daughter of Michael and Catherine Snyder.

she was attempting to take it. Apparently, Alta wanted to control the family fortune and was not above legal action when she believed someone to be making ill use of his or her portion. Although it is still a quiet topic within the family, in one case, Alta was not pleased with the way one deceased member willed their money. Even though the will dictated that the monetary estate was to be divided among several family members, Alta believed it should all have been left to her. Albeit inconceivable, she was actually able to bully all but one of the beneficiaries into giving their inheritance to her. Not content with less than the whole, however, Alta eventually took the holdout to court. Realizing that her case was weak, it is commonly said that Alta actually bought off the judge and, in a stunning victory, was awarded the final portion of the estate. In the end, the incident seems to truly give new meaning to the saying "It takes money to make money"!

On a lighter note, it is frequently said that Alta Snyder also had an incredible sense of humor. One senior member of the community recalls that, as a child, one of the only reasons she liked to visit the Snyders was because Alta was so funny. Additionally, this youngster also found entertainment in the fact that Alta was so short that her feet didn't touch the ground when she sat in a chair. It's comforting to know that everyone has their good points.

Abraham Lincoln Snyder

Regarding the married Snyder children, family records indicate that Abraham Lincoln Snyder married Grace M. Dryer (1870–1947) and lived on the northeast corner of Main Street and Chateau Terrace. The couple had one daughter, Edna (Broadbrooks), who eventually married and moved to Rochester. From his father's example, Abraham learned the necessary skills to be an auctioneer and practiced this professionally for a number of years. On the outside, a cursory glance of the lives of Abe and Grace Snyder showed them to be relatively quiet and simple folk. As if it hadn't become clear enough with the other siblings, however, nothing about this generation was ever as normal as it seemed. Beneath this common appearance, Abraham's life had also bred its share of scandal. Apparently, Abraham Snyder was married twice. In his first marriage, Abe wed Ella Peterson and had two children, Arthur (?–1905) and Florence (1886–1909). After the loss of his first wife, Abraham decided to remarry. When he proposed to Grace Dryer, however, she indicated that she would consent to be his wife but not the mother of his two children. It was at this point that Abe decided to give his children to his parents so that he could marry Grace. Michael and Catherine

Abraham Snyder's backyard encompassed the Chateau Terrace property now owned by Bornhava Preschool. Pictured are Abraham Snyder, his niece Viola Wannenwetch and nephew Bobby Fiddler.

then legally adopted Arthur and Florence and cared for them until the onset of their untimely deaths. Unfortunately, they both died as teenagers, with Arthur passing in 1905 and Florence in 1909.

Elma Amanda Snyder

Elma Snyder was the first and only sibling to eventually leave the Snyder area. In a secret ceremony, Elma Snyder married Aden Miller, who originally hailed from Clarence, New York. Aden was not only a local wheelwright; he was also the Snyders' first cousin. In their early years, the couple lived in the house next to the Beck building on Harlem Road. Together, Elma and Aden had several children: Maude, Elmer, Olga, Raymond, Blanche and Olive. Increasingly aware of the family's disapproval of the union, however, Elma and Aden disappeared while the children were still young. Reportedly, the couple fled to St. Louis, where they eventually joined a wagon train and headed for California. In company with both immigrant peasants and headstrong pioneers, Elma's wagon train ultimately settled on the Oregon Trail. About twenty years after the tragedy that befell the Donner party, Elma and her fellow travelers arrived safely on the white sands of the California coast. Although she and her husband never returned to the Snyder area,

Located on the east side of Harlem, just south of Main Street, this house was rented by Elma Snyder Miller following her marriage.

all of their children made visits back home. Eventually, although each of the Millers' children would marry and have children of their own, the close genetic ties of their parents would interfere in their personal lives. As is often the case with same family marriages, all of the Miller children were emotionally unstable and two, Olive and Blanche, died in mental institutions. In 1934, Elma Snyder Miller died in Los Angeles, California, far from her family and her hometown.

Solomon Sherman Snyder

Finally, Solomon Sherman Snyder married Caroline LeBrun (1872–1931) and had three daughters. During his spare time he enjoyed several hobbies, such as playing drums in a band and volunteering at the Snyder Hose Company. Remarkably, there does not seem to be anything even remotely odd about Solomon, his hobbies or his family. As a young man he met and married Caroline, who was also a Snyder native. Caroline's family, it is reported, owned a farm about a mile west of Harlem Road on the south side of Main

Street. Eventually, a road was paved through the estate and christened LeBrun Road in the family's honor. Today, the road exists as a posh residential area and is frequently considered one of the finest neighborhoods in the Snyder vicinity. In 1902, Solomon and Caroline Snyder moved into the old band hall building and converted it to a home marked 4464 Main Street. Even once it was established as a residence, the home maintained the genre of the historic hall. Reminders were evident in the large, open rooms, thick plaster walls and long, thin windows. Each room was also characterized by excessively tall ceilings, originally meant to provide better acoustics. By the early 1900s, indoor plumbing was also common to most people. Solomon Snyder, however, flatly refused to take part in this revolution. According to his daughter Agnes, her father only agreed to install indoor plumbing after quite a few years of prodding by his wife and daughters. As part of this compromise, the facilities were established in the far rear of the house. By this placement, Solomon reasoned that he could still maintain his simple lifestyle. It was unfortunate, however, that the only way to reach this section of the house was via an unheated hallway. In the winter, ice would actually form on the inside walls. In later years, Solomon's granddaughter Viola frequently joked as to the raw courage it took to brave the trip to the bathroom on a cold winter night.

Solomon and Caroline (LeBrun) Snyder. After their marriage, the Snyders would convert the old Snyder band hall into a home and raise three daughters there.

Nevertheless, it was in this green plank house that the Snyders raised three daughters. Their oldest, Agnes Catherine (1892–1991), married Louis Wannenwetsch and, by 1927, was expecting their first child. Unfortunately, as was common in those days, Agnes suffered major complications during the birth of their child. The doctors soon emerged from the delivery room and asked Louis to make an impossible decision. Not confident that both mother and child could survive this most difficult labor, Louis was asked to choose between the life of his wife and his new baby. Watching Louis struggle so desperately with this decision, the doctor mentioned a "new" surgical procedure that was currently being tested on expectant mothers. He explained how a fetus could actually be surgically removed from a woman's uterus and both mother and baby were known to survive. He then reported that the hospital had never performed this type of delivery before and the procedure was highly suspect. Unable to live with the prospect of voluntarily losing his wife or child, Louis consented to a procedure that, doctors warned him, could kill them both. With eight doctors presiding over the surgery, Agnes Snyder Wannenwetsch soon delivered Viola Carolyn via the first Cesarean section in Millard Fillmore Hospital.

Soon thereafter, Agnes lost her mother and the following appeared in the *Amherst Bee* dated July 9, 1931:

> *After suffering with ill health for several years, Mrs. Solomon S. Snyder entered into eternal rest Thursday morning, July 2, 1931, aged 59 years. She was the daughter of Eugene and Sophia LeBrun. Her family was one well known here in the early years, and it has been perpetuated by the designation of an important thoroughfare in the Eggertsville section where the homestead was, as "LeBrun Road."*

Following her father's death in 1934, Agnes and Louie inherited the refurbished band hall and proudly raised their daughter Viola within its walls. Regardless of the year, history could come alive inside this green plank house. Seventy years after its conversion to a home, Agnes would continue to open the front door to tourists and schoolchildren who wanted to capture some of the nostalgia locked inside. As time passed, however, the eminent demise of 4464 Main Street was a necessary, yet disturbing, event. Over one hundred years after its construction, the house stood as the last reminder of Michael Snyder's handiwork. In between doctors' offices, fur shops and fancy clothing stores, the house retained its dignity in a town that literally grew around it. Unfortunately, with Agnes's health failing and relatives

An early 1920s photograph of Beulah Snyder, relaxing over Ellicott Creek. At that time, the creek ran above ground near Getzville Road.

The residence of Abraham Lincoln Snyder on the northeast corner of Main Street and Chateau Terrace, presently Bomi jewelers.

unable to take responsibility for preserving the landmark, 4464 Main Street was vacated in the late 1980s. With no fanfare, TV cameras or reporters, a building that had entertained five generations of Snyders came to exist only in memories, news clippings and old photo albums. In the end, an era that took over one hundred years to create took workmen less than one day to reduce to dust.

While her sister lived her whole life in the band hall, my grandmother, Beulah Sophia Snyder (1895–1957), liked to travel the country. Even before her marriage to Earl Fiddler (1901–1964) on August 20, 1927, Beulah's photo albums depict a life of worthy of the Roaring Twenties. Traveling with her pack of friends, Beulah documents trips from Washington, D.C., to Canada and proudly displays one crazy pose after another. Following their marriage, Beulah and Earl enjoyed short stays on North Harlem Road, the farmlands of Bennington and the city life on Humboldt Parkway in Buffalo. Finally returning to Snyder seventeen years later, the Fiddlers and their children Robert (1930–1986) and Ruth (1932–   ) eventually settled in Abraham and Grace Snyder's old house on the northeast corner of Main Street and Chateau Terrace. It was here that Beulah Snyder Fiddler penned many of the charming memories scattered throughout this book.

Taken by Beulah Snyder Fiddler, this view from 127 Hamilton Drive looks north toward Kings Highway and Coolidge Drive. Pictured is Bobby Fiddler.

The youngest of the Snyder sisters, Gladys Rose Snyder (1902–1994), was affectionately known as "Toodles" to her family and friends. Standing all of four feet, eight inches tall, Gladys was never far from a silly story or a tall tale. Whether she was inadvertently getting into "hot water" somewhere or accidentally sitting on her pet canary, Gladys had the ability to make her life seem like a vaudeville act. In her younger years, Toodles spent a great deal of time traveling with her sister Beulah. As evidenced by the photos, the Snyder sisters were living proof that the gilded age of the 1920s was truly a roaring era. In a manner of which even F. Scott Fitzgerald could be proud, it seems as if Gladys and Beulah lived every tale from *This Side of Paradise* to *Bernice Bobs Her Hair*. Whether on the beach or in the snow up to their waists, their pictorial essay beautifully documents a time of innocence and fortune. Having fallen in love during one of her annual jaunts to Owasko Lake, however, Gladys Snyder unpacked her suitcase in 1935 and married Edward Church (1903–1977) of Syracuse. Having no children and losing her husband at a young age, Gladys eventually returned to the Snyder area and lived on Hamilton Drive. Mirroring the longevity known to the Snyder family, Auntie Gladys lived in Snyder until the ripe old age of ninety-one.

CHAPTER FIVE

Founding Families

From Pioneers to Prominent Businessmen

Pioneer Families

During these years, the Snyders were by no means the only successful family in the hamlet. After purchasing the Hopkins estate and opening the mercantile with his cousin Michael Snyder, John Schenck and his family began to increase their stature in the community. Tragedy struck, however, when the original stone house on the Schencks' property was destroyed by fire. It was then that the spirit of this new community came together and John Schenck, with the help of his new neighbors and friends, built a very fine brick house in its place. In a testimony to the self-efficiency of this new hamlet, the handmade brick for the estate came from a new Snyder brickyard on Harlem Road just south of Main Street.

Along with the Snyders, the Schenck family became major landholders in the new hamlet and eventually erected a small stone house farther north down Harlem Road. This timeless piece of history still stands on the busy road, valiantly perched at the entrance to the prestigious Park School of Buffalo. Throughout its lifetime, this tiny building has served many functions, including providing residence for early families, serving as the Snyder Museum of Natural History and being part of the Park School's grounds. No function is more noteworthy, however, than the pervasive notion that this house was a fixture of the Underground Railroad. By all accounts, Quakers from Orchard Park would accompany the runaway slaves to the Schencks' stone house. Here, they could hide, eat and rest before making the final fifteen-mile journey into Canada.

In 1958, William Shaver photographed the demolition of the Schenck estate at the southeast corner of Main Street and Amherstdale Road, presently Denny's Restaurant.

Originally owned by the Schenck family, the stone house on Harlem Road has served as a local museum and a stop on the Underground Railroad.

In this sole act, the Snyder area carved itself a rich piece of classic American history.

Alongside the Snyders and Schencks, several other families began to live and work in Snyderville. Some early names about the hamlet were Freuhauf, Helfter, LeBrun, Miller, Fischer, Schuler, Cable, Witmer, Beck, Crout, Harrison, Kern, Frick and Fogelsonger. Over time, these names helped to expand the village into a prosperous and self-sufficient unit. Although as the years passed this quaint hamlet would both grow and change, over 150 years later, the village of Snyder still exists as a spectacular living tribute to these brave and energetic souls.

Records indicate that the first hotel in the Snyder area was opened and operated by the Kern family. The Kern Hotel stood in the general vicinity of our present Daemen College and served a wide variety of travelers. As time passed, however, the Kerns made the decision to move on and turned operation of this hotel over to the Becks. Ironically, it seems as if this transaction took place just before Snyderville truly began to grow. Regardless, in 1882, L.F. Crout seized the opportunity to open a competitive hotel and attached a fully functional saloon as a marketing incentive.

The Maple Grove Inn, originally owned by the Harris family. After burning to the ground, the property was sold to the Gardner family.

Taken in front of 4344 Harlem Road, the Beck building is visible on the south corner and Helfter's can be seen across Main Street.

Whether as a result of this new competition or for more personal reasons, the Becks soon relinquished the management of their hotel to the Harrison family. After being bought by the Harrisons, the old hotel operated for a short time but eventually burned to the ground. Opting not to rebuild the business, the Harrisons sold the property to the Gardners, who would build a most prestigious estate.

In the meantime, the Becks began to operate a novelty store on the southeast corner of Main Street and Harlem Road. This store, which doubled as the Becks' homestead, remains one of the only original Snyderville buildings still in existence. When the old Socony Gasoline Station was erected, however, the entire building was moved farther south on Harlem Road in order to make room. According to longtime proprietor of the Snyder Pharmacy, Martin Quinn, this process was very interesting to watch. Although only a youngster at the time, Mr. Quinn recalls how the movers picked up the north-facing house and turned it west in an effort to have the entrance on Harlem Road. They then placed the building on a new stone foundation. Currently, the original Beck building stands behind the Mobil "On the Run" Station. A brilliantly large yellow building, the

The original Fischer Bros. Mr. Schuckler (fourth from right), young Pat Fischer (fifth from right), Otto Schuler (third from left) and Charles Snyder (first on left)

Beck homestead is leased as office space, yet it maintains most of the original characteristics from the outside view.

Looking down the south side of Main Street, one would find a rug weaving establishment in the vicinity of Lincoln Drive and a brickyard on the south side of Harlem Road. To the west of Harlem Road, the first flour mill in the area was located near Berryman Drive. On the north side of Main Street, a small pottery factory existed across from the Schenck estate. A few hundred feet east, the Fischers operated a general store and attached saloon.

There, they also maintained their homestead with a series of barns and sheds. A prominent and popular family in the hamlet, the Fischer brothers produced signage that boasted "bailed hay and oats, prompt delivery" on one building and "Flour, Feed, Etc" on another. The Fischers endured their fair share of hardships, including losing their store in the fire of 1905, but always bounced back with the help of their friends and neighbors. By December 1907, the Fischers were back on their feet, but one of their employees, it seems, was not so lucky. According to an *Amherst Bee* article dated December 19, 1907, "William Shuler of Williamsville, an employee of Fischer Bros. of Snyder, lost his balance while unloading grain at August Baetzhold's on Michigan Street in Buffalo, falling backward and landing on his head."

A view of the Fischer Bros. new store, looking east down Main Street between Harlem Road and Chateau Terrace.

On the north side of Main Street, Jacob Freuhauf operated a large farm in the vicinity of the road that is now named in his honor. Eventually, Freuhauf went into the meat business and then spent twenty-two years in the flour, feed and grocery business. Advertisements of the time boasted this establishment to be "a first class store for farmers and others...an excellent stock of goods to sell at the lowest prices." Tragedy struck in 1881, however, as fire spread from a nearby barn, badly damaging the Freuhaufs' property. More importantly, Jacob Freuhauf, who was standing near the barn as it caught ablaze, suffered burns to his face.

At this time, limestone was quarried at two Snyderville locations. In the heart of the village, a small quarry operated near the Schenck estate on the corner of Main Street and Amherstdale Road. Eventually, the Decot family would buy the quarry's property and erect a large yellow brick house. Presently, this property is part of the Snyder branch of the YMCA. The largest quarry, however, was located on the north side of Main Street near Park Club Lane. The quarried land was owned by John Fogelsonger, and at that time, Park Club Lane was known as Fogelsonger Road in his honor. Amid the limestone on the Folgelsongers' estate, there also existed a large sulphur spring. In the early years, John harnessed the power from this spring and operated a successful three-story gristmill. It wasn't until 1852 that his son Wendell opened the quarries in an effort to supply limestone for local construction and ballast for the railroads. A very successful enterprise, the only noted tragedy occurred in 1879 when the Folgelsongers' lime kilns violently burned to the ground. In the 1950s, New York State would disband Folgelsonger's quarry and run the New York State Thruway through the quarry's depths. With this in mind, the next time you travel the walkway of the 290 overpass, take a minute to stop and gaze into the canyon that generations of Snyderville men threw pick and axe to carve. The next time you drive your car past the chiseled thruway walls, you can look up from the depths of the old quarry and, for a moment, trade places with one of those lost and forgotten quarrymen.

On the opposite side of Main Street, past Getzvill, the Berrymans and LeBruns were early farming families who lent their names to modern-day neighborhoods. On the south side of Main Street, well past Harlem Road, each operated successful farms and orchards. The LeBruns, it seems, were a most notable addition to the Snyder area. In addition to their successful farming operation, their daughter, Caroline, would eventually marry Michael

In 1906, the Fischers opened a new two-story general store to replace the building lost in the fire of 1905. *Courtesy of the Snyder Fire Department.*

Occupying the 1906 Fischer Bros. building, Wilkies was located on the north side of Main Street next to Shorty Ludwig's garage. *Courtesy of the Snyder Fire Department.*

Snyder's son, Solomon. Although their connection to the Snyder family is notable, the LeBruns stemmed from a fascinating lineage of their own. Although the mention of the family name may mean little in twenty-first-century America, it once held great power in seventeenth-century France. In an interesting twist of fate, it is known that the LeBruns' ancestor, Charles LeBrun (1619–1690), was none other than first painter to King Louis XIV.

One of the first French artist-politicians, Charles LeBrun was known for his gigantic paintings and preliminary designs for many famous pieces of art. In 1647, Charles LeBrun exhibited an altarpiece for Notre Dame that spawned his tremendous success as an artist and designer. Widely considered the best in his field, Charles LeBrun was employed by King Louis XIV for the construction of the palace at Versailles. Working under his protector Colbert, Charles assumed overall responsibility for the painting and sculptural decoration of Versailles' chateau and park. Aside from providing his own artwork for decoration, LeBrun also provided drawings for "executant" painters and sculptures. Among his renowned executants at Versailles were Francois Girardon, Pierre LeGros, the Marsy brothers (Gasphard and Balthazar), Guido Reni, Jean Cotelle the Younger and Antoine Coysevox. Undeniably, LeBrun's most famous executant at Versailles was sculptor Jean Baptiste Tuby. Tuby sculpted many of LeBrun's designs, including *Puti with a*

Swan, *Flora* (one of the *Four Seasons*) and the infamous *Apollo Fountain*, and one of the premier artworks of this project.

Inside the palace, LeBrun is credited with the decoration of several chambers, including the Salon de la Guerre and the Salon de la Paix, each complete in 1686. His most famous chamber, however, is the Galerie des Glaces or the Hall of Mirrors, which he decorated from 1679 to 1684. Constructed for King Louis XIV's state functions, the hall is said to be the largest chamber at the palace and the epitome of the artistry at Versailles.

Beyond the palace at Versailles, Charles LeBrun's work can be enjoyed at a number of galleries in countries worldwide. While still in France, one can find approximately two thousand of LeBrun's paintings and drawings on display at the Louvre. Charles LeBrun was actually one of the three men to design the east façade of the Louvre building itself. Coincidentally, there is also a sculpture bust of Charles LeBrun inside the Louvre, submitted by Antoine Coysevox in 1679. Other LeBrun works can be found in London, Montreal, Bristol, Munich, Nottingham, Ottawa, Stockholm, Prague and Venice. Closer to home, LeBrun's original drawings for *Puti with a Swan* and *Puti with a Lyre* (sculpted at Versailles by Tuby and LeGros) are on display in the National Gallery of Art in Washington, D.C. During his career, Charles LeBrun had the honor of being named chancellor of the Royal Academy of Painting and Sculpture, director of the Academy of St. Luke in Rome, director of the Gobelins and dictator of the arts under King Louis XIV. For the French Academy, LeBrun implemented a strict system of rules and complemented it with a treatise on the "expression of the passions."

The LeBrun family and its descendants remained in France for the next few centuries. By the nineteenth century, however, the marriage of Caroline's parents had mandated the family's migration to America. Apparently, Caroline's mother, Sophia, was a native of Germany as well as a German citizen. When she and Jean Nicholas (Eugene) LeBrun fell in love, the union was severely frowned upon by both family and country. But their love proved stronger than either tie, and the couple was united in marriage. Following the union, Jean Nicholas and his new bride attempted to endure the enormous ethnic prejudice that soon ensued. Their valor notwithstanding, the couple soon fled the tumult and immigrated to America. Deciding to settle in the growing Snyder area, the LeBruns purchased a large farm and cultivated it successfully for a number of years. Finally, upon settling in Snyder, the couple had several children, one of whom was Caroline LeBrun Snyder.

THE *AMHERST BEE*

Although headquartered in the village of Williamsville, the *Amherst Bee* has remained a staple of community news since the late 1800s. Conceived by Adam L. Reinwalt, the *Amherst Bee* opened in a small building next to the famous Mansion House on Main Street. Using a hand press, on March 27, 1879, the inaugural issue was born. As it continued as a weekly paper, Reinwalt served as publisher and Marvin Reist came aboard as the first editor. The first issue published its subscription price, one dollar per year in advance, and its subscription, news and editorial policies. On page two appeared the following introduction:

> *Friends and anxious patron of the BEE, we humbly make our appearance and with the kindest greetings to all, we send forth our first number. Stimulated by the spirit of progress, and being desirous to promote and maintain a kindly feeling between the different factions of this town, the BEE has adopted a domain peculiar to itself, and is concerned with matters the most interesting to the town, people and friends. We shall endeavor to accurately report, rather than create, so that the BEE will be regarded as the index of the social life of the village and surroundings.*

Without question, the *Amherst Bee* continued to live up to the high goals set for it, and as circulation increased, the printing of the *Bee* required more power. Acquiring a new press driven by "horse power," which consisted of a single horse walking in a circle, the paper's production moved to a basement on the northeast corner of Main and North Cayuga Streets. The production facilities also made a brief stop on a site near St. Peter and Paul's Church before moving into its permanent home on the corner of Main and Rock Streets.

By 1907, the very successful *Amherst Bee* was purchased by George J. Measer and his brother Frank A. Measer, who left the business shortly thereafter. Following his marriage to Eugenie Snyder that same year, George had two sons, Robert Snyder and George J. Jr., and thus began the Measers' legacy at the *Amherst Bee*. Following his death in 1965, the weekly paper was attended to by his son, George Jr., followed by his son Trey and his son Michael. In 2009, the Measer family is still firmly in charge of the *Amherst Bee* and proudly maintains the *Bee*'s 130-year history of never missing a weekly issue. The most impressive of these would have to be the paper that came out during the Blizzard of 1977. Working with a skeleton staff, the *Amherst Bee* managed to put together its weekly edition. Although skinnier than usual, the staff had accomplished something that many other larger and more prestigious papers could not.

Thus, for the last 130 years, the *Amherst Bee* has provided the people of Amherst with everything from important news to playful fodder. An institution in its own right, the *Bee* is a living part of our history and continuously connects the people of today to the people who made today possible.

THE TURN OF THE TWENTIETH CENTURY

The dawn of the twentieth century was an exciting time around the world. In 1900, Paris hosted the Summer Olympics, officially known as the Games of the II Olympiad, and in 1901, Buffalo captured the world's attention during the Pan American Exposition. While the tragic assassination of William McKinley rocked Buffalo and the suburbs, Theodore Roosevelt was inaugurated at 641 Delaware Avenue. Scientifically, this period of time saw the invention of the vacuum cleaner in 1901, the air conditioner in 1902 and the first powered flight by the Wright brothers in 1903. Reginald Fessenden pioneered radio broadcasting in 1906 and wives marveled at the debut of the electric washing machine in 1907. On Broadway, George M.

A 1931 scene from the Fischers' house shows one of their children (standing left) playing with Viola Wannenwetch (standing right) and Bobby Fiddler (on pony).

Cohan summoned up the nation's pride with his 1904 smash hit *Little Johnny Jones*, in which he unveiled his timeless classics "Yankee Doodle Dandy" and "Give My Regards to Broadway." Two years later, in his Broadway hit *George Washington Jr.*, Cohan would capture the hearts of the nation as he sang his new hit, "You're a Grand Old Flag."

By 1900, the village of Snyder boasted about three dozen families and by 1901, electric lights had been installed down Main Street. It seems that as Snyder grew and transportation improved, this prominent suburb became a popular destination for some of Buffalo's successful businessmen. Taking full advantage of the Toonerville Trolley, one of the first to leave the city in search of Snyder's "rural" beauty was Arthur E. Hedstrom, president of Hedstrom-Spaulding. One of Buffalo's largest coal dealers, Hedstrom was a civic leader and wealthy man when he purchased over one hundred acres of Snyder land in 1904. Born in 1869, Hedstrom was an active leader of the Buffalo YMCA, where he was a member of the board of directors from 1900 to 1926 and of the board of trustees from 1920 to 1932. As a member of the Buffalo Country Club, he was also a seasoned golfer who represented Buffalo at the Tournament of the Lower Lakes in Rochester on July 17–18, 1909. According to *American Golfer Magazine* (1909), Toronto, Detroit, Cleveland, Buffalo and Rochester were slated to be represented at this prestigious tournament. Also named to the five-person team that would represent Buffalo was fellow Snyder resident Allen Gardner.

Sprawling across the west side of Getzville Road, the impressive grounds of Hedstrom's new one-hundred-acre estate extended from Main Street to the Freuhaufs' property on Sheridan Drive and were enclosed by a stately stone wall. Included in the purchase were the old tollgate keeper's house as well as a farmhouse, barn and shed used by earlier farmers. After his marriage to Katherine Wilcox, Hedstrom planned to renovate the estate and hired architect Frederick Loverin, who had previously designed the Lenox Hotel on North Street in Buffalo. Although his wife had originally wanted her sister Mable to live in the main house with them, Hedstrom had other ideas and entrusted Loverin to renovate the west barn house for Mable instead. While redesigning both the east and west buildings, Loverin decided to bring up the shed, raise the roofline and pull the fronts of the homes out, enabling the second floors to hang over the first. To cap off his Tudor Revival masterpiece, Loverin then added dormers to the front. It is important to note that pieces of the original dismantled tollgate may also have been included in the design, being incorporated into the archway used to connect the east and west buildings.

HOMES ON A. E. HEDSTROM ESTATES, MAIN STREET, Snyder, N. Y.

A past view of the gatehouse properties on Main Street and Getzville Road. *Courtesy of Caroline Duax.*

A present view of the gatehouse properties on Main Street and Getzville Road.

In the end, Hedstrom had erected a stunning stone mansion and accented it with a row of caretaker cottages. The old barn had been converted to a carriage house and a new state-of-the-art barn was constructed behind the gatehouse. A riding stable was also attached to the carriage house and stately stone archways led visitors to the grassy areas. The park-like grounds were adorned with gardens, an orchard and a skating pond. The estate also boasted one of Snyder's first pools and a luxurious pool house. Upon completion, the property was affectionately named Four Winds Farm.

The country club atmosphere and friendly company endeared the Hedstroms and their estate as a favorite destination for the Snyder family as well as all of the Amherst townsfolk. In 1908, the *Amherst Bee* proudly reported, "Mr. and Mrs. Arthur E. Hedstrom entertained the choir of the Delaware Avenue Baptist Church at their home in Snyder." In fact, tales of skating parties and horseback riding can still be heard among the senior residents of the community. In total, the Hedstroms remained at this estate for forty-three years and had three children. Although they lost an infant in 1912, their son Eric II and daughter Brenda Hedstrom lived long and happy lives. In fact, when daughter Brenda married Mr. Boocock from the adjacent Four Winds Nursery, the Hedstroms gave them a brown shingled colonial house, presently on Getzville Road, as well as part of their property as a wedding present.

A past view of the stone mansion of Arthur Hedstrom, located on the extensive property behind the gatehouse. *Courtesy of Caroline Duax.*

A present view of the stone mansion of Arthur Hedstrom, presently accessed from Getzville Road and hidden behind town houses.

In 1949, having lost her husband Arthur three years prior, Katherine Wilcox Hedstrom sold the entire estate to Genrich Builders, which developed much of the land and converted the gatehouse for commercial use. Presently nestled behind an array of new town homes, the Hedstroms' stone mansion still stands off Getzville Road. Hidden from the street, the mansion maintains its outward dignity but has been divided several times internally to create a spread of apartments. Farther down Getzville, quietly tucked off Elmhurst, Hedstrom's pond also survives and greets visitors with a glimpse of the quiet country life that the Hedstoms' visitors once enjoyed.

In 2002, 1.6 acres of the Hedstroms' land, which included the gatehouse, carriage house and the infamous stone wall, received historical designation. When viewing from Main Street, sightseers will notice trees to the left of the west barn house that date back to 1810. The east house is believed to have been built between 1840 and 1850 and still contains original posts and beams that corroborate this date. It is also possible that past architects incorporated signature pieces of the original Main Street Tollgate into the

Beulah Snyder Fiddler captured a skating party on Hedstrom's Pond in the early 1920s.

With the Hedstroms' property sold and divided, Hedstrom's Pond now lies on Elmhurst Drive, accessed from Getzville Road.

unique archway connecting these structures. Although it is mere speculation, it is nevertheless exciting to hope that one of Snyder's most precious pieces of history may still be alive inside the structure. In 2006, the Duax family purchased the property and has worked tirelessly to restore the estate to much of its original grandeur. Thanks to their efforts, a century after its creation, the Hedstroms' stone wall will continue to greet those who travel the corner of Main Street and Getzville Road and will stand as testimony to the happy times and precious memories made behind it.

By 1911, the Hedstroms had a new neighbor by the name of Herbert Crouch. A general agent of the Northwest Mutual Life Insurance Company, Crouch purchased twenty-three acres on the east side of Getzville Road. Employing famed Buffalo architect George Cary, the Crouches built a unique mansion adorned with a garage and a penthouse. The grand estate also displayed landscaped gardens, fruit orchards, horse stables and a prestigious swan lake.

In 1912, after acquiring the land on which the Kern Hotel originally stood, Allen Gardner built a most prestigious estate north of Main Street, between Getzville and Harlem Roads. The Gardner family stemmed from a

The site of the great robbery of Amherst, the Gardner/Carson mansion now serves as Rosary Hall on the Daemen College campus. *Photo by Peter Scumaci.*

prominent family tree, including Gayer Gardner, who was wounded during the Battle of Fricksburg in the Civil War, and Joseph Gardner, who developed the commercial harbor in Buffalo. Although the Gardners' property held many treasures, the showpiece of the estate was the graceful Georgian-style mansion in which the family lived. The main foyer was adorned with black marble flooring, a vaulted ceiling and ornamental staircase. The rooms boasted elliptical windows and enjoyed carved marble mantels atop five fireplaces. The roof was made of custom blue-glazed tiles, and a series of French doors led to the well-manicured grounds outside. Although the Gardner family enjoyed several years in their glamorous Snyder estate, the house and grounds were sold to the Carson family in the 1920s.

It was in the Carsons' house in 1929 that one of Snyder's most enduring criminal tales took place: the Great Robbery of Amherst. In November 1929, the Carsons were hosting a dinner party at the estate for eighteen unsuspecting guests. According to legend, the third-course dinner had just been served when seven uninvited guests burst into the room. The intruders wore handkerchief masks on their faces but appeared to have no weapons. The Snyder natives, who were unaccustomed to such "Billy the Kid" types of crimes, assumed the seven men to be friends of the host. Thinking that the robbery attempt was nothing more than a Wild West practical joke, the party began to laugh at the bandits' demands. Furious, one of the masked men knocked down the host and began to kick him. As the rest of the party realized the seriousness of the situation, they instinctively attempted to subdue the thieves. Less prepared for the battle, however, they too were beaten and kicked to the floor. In the pandemonium of combat, one female guest quickly escaped and concealed her diamonds. By the time the thieves approached her, she evidenced no sign of valuable property.

Once the seven masked bandits had overthrown the dinner guests, they seated them about the table and held them at gunpoint. While one held a revolver, the outlaws ripped the jewelry from the women and stripped the men of their shirt studs and valuables. Then, while a few of the masked men stayed to guard the victims, the others proceeded to the upstairs rooms to gather the ladies' fur coats. The household goods, incidentally, were left unscathed. Following the robbers' departure, the Carsons notified the authorities. Without any of the guests being able to identify the perpetrators, however, the case remained unsolved.

By the late 1940s, the Carsons sold their estate to the Sisters of St. Francis and it became part of the new Rosary Hill College. During the school's early years, the original mansion house, now called Rosary Hall, contained the entire college. As Rosary Hill grew into Daemen College, Rosary Hall was designated as an administrative building. Following extensive renovations to bring the structure back to its original glory, Rosary Hall presently showcases many of the original aesthetic features and ornaments of the Gardners' home.

As development continued, David and Joseph Coplon, who hailed from one of Western New York's oldest and most prominent Jewish families, purchased the property next door and began construction at the northeast corner of Main Street and Getzville Road. The Coplons were a well-known family, owning a successful furniture chain and becoming prominent members of the Western New York community. Employing the architectural styles of the fifteenth century, the Coplon brothers chose to build a mansion where they could still live their separate lives. The resulting masterpiece had a wing for each brother and was connected by a living hall and loggia. The estate also included a separate and more modest apartment for their mother, Rosa Coplon. Although she only lived in Snyder a short while before her death, Rosa had already established quite a name for herself in the Western New York community at large. As a result of her pioneering efforts in the nursing home field, the new Jewish Home and Infirmary in Buffalo's Symphony Circle was named in her honor. The Coplons' original mansion still proudly stands as part of Daemen College and serves as Patricia E. Curtis Hall,

Captured here by Beulah Snyder in the early 1920s, the Coplon mansion now serves as Curtis Hall on the Daemen College campus.

which houses physician assistant, psychology and social work faculty offices, as well as the Honors Program. Rosa Coplon's apartment also serves the college as an adjacent maintenance building.

Northwest of the Gardner and Coplon estates, attorney Chauncey Hamlin, who was active in the formation of the Reformist Progressive Party, built his own impressive estate on Harlem Road. Located on the property were five buildings, an apple orchard, grain fields, a brook, two ponds and mounds of lilacs and forsythias. Included among the buildings was the old Schenck stone house on Harlem Road. This, Hamlin decided, would be a perfect spot for him to create the Snyder Museum of Natural History. In it, he housed a collection of natural objects that he and his children had excavated from his property. In a more regional effort, Hamlin was also instrumental in the creation of the Buffalo Museum of Science. In 1912, the Hamlins' property was sold and the Park School of Buffalo was opened on the grounds.

CHAPTER SIX

FIRE!

The Snyderville Fires and the Birth of the Snyder Hose Company

Prior to the twentieth century, fire was one of the most threatening and ominous enemies a town could face. The practice of organized fire departments was less than common and an adequate water supply was frequently impossible due to limited technology of the time. Within a twenty-five-year span, this enemy's flame entered the tiny hamlet of Snyder twice and ignited two very powerful and devastating fires.

THE FIRE OF 1881

Although one usually pictures a raging fire taking place in the warmer months, the fire of 1881 began on a cold December day. Bred from an uncertain origin, sources say that the fire first began in a barn owned by Frank Wittig on the north side of Main Street, a few hundred yards east of Harlem Road. Compliments of the icy December wind, the flames soon spread to the Wittigs' nearby blacksmith shop. Despite the efforts of the Wittigs and the Freuhaufs, the Wittigs' next-door neighbors, both buildings were soon destroyed. In fact, the December winds soon carried burning embers to the Freuhaufs' barn. Recognizing the potential magnitude of this blaze, efforts quickly turned to saving the Freuhaufs' other properties. Most importantly, the Freuhaufs operated a general store on the northeast corner of Main Street and what is now named Freuhauf Drive in their honor. The townsfolk and their rudimentary "bucket brigade," however, were no match for the winter blaze. Despite valiant efforts, several buildings of both the Wittigs and the Freuhaufs were ravaged. The estimated losses, given in dollar values of the time, were approximately $400 for each family. Bear in mind, however, that there was no fire insurance to cover the damage. On top of that, the families were responsible for an estimate $45 in property lost to Aden Miller. At that time, Aden, a first cousin of the Snyders, was a working wheelwright who stored property in one of the barns destroyed in the blaze. In the end, the cause of the fire was traced to children playing with matches.

In hindsight, the village of Snyder was probably indebted to the dreary December weather this region is so famous for. If a fire of this magnitude had been given warm air to breed in and dry ground to travel upon, the effects of this blaze could have been colossal. Although it seems ridiculous to consider this devastation fortunate, it pales in comparison to the embers that awaited illumination in 1905.

THE FIRE OF 1905

At approximately five o'clock one hot July afternoon, fire broke out in George Helfter's barn, site of the blacksmith shop built by Michael Snyder. Although the townsfolk worked quickly to form a bucket brigade, the roof was soon ablaze and burning embers had ignited his nearby wagon works. The fire's path continued to the Fischers' property, catching their sheds, icehouse and grain-filled barns. The grain fed the fire rapidly and the Fischer Bros.' two-story general store and Helfter's homestead soon burned violently. A call was placed to the Buffalo Fire Headquarters and the crew arrived in a record-setting twenty minutes. Together, the Buffalo Firefighters and Snyder townspeople continued to battle the fire with water from nearby wells and cisterns. Since there was no formal water system in the Snyder Village, however, the supply soon depleted. Without water, energies turned to rescuing furniture and possessions. Reportedly, the firemen and townspeople would enter the burning buildings and carry valuable items to the road for salvation. In Beulah Snyder Fiddler's notes, she recalls a grand piano standing in the middle of Main Street. Unfortunately, she also explains how petty thieving was common during such a crisis. In fact, Beulah reported that, besides losing her store and homestead to the fire, Mrs. Fischer also had her best hat stolen in the confusion. Beulah was aghast!

As the catastrophe escalated, so did the wind. As it quickly changed direction, embers soared across Main Street and ignited Joseph Beck's Grocery and sheds at the southeast corner of Harlem Road. Another

The fire of 1905 ravaged the hamlet, reducing thirteen of the village's buildings to ashes. This photo is believed to show the Fischers' property. *Courtesy of the Snyder Fire Department.*

burning ember was carried nearly 1,500 feet west to the Schenck barn on the opposite corner. Farther west, the Kabel barn also caught fire. Remarkably, the Schenck homestead in between their barn and Kabel's was spared.

Within two hours, most of Snyderville's business district, twelve buildings in all, was reduced to ashes. Ironically, none of the Snyder family property was touched by the calamity. In fact, it is rumored that the Snyder homestead, post office and band hall were the only unscathed buildings in Snyderville. Following the disaster, the fire department reported that with enough water, most of the buildings could have been saved. Ironically, a short time earlier, the local water company had offered to install hydrants in the Snyder community. At a price of sixty dollars apiece, however, the frugal community deemed the venture too expensive and rejected the offer. One can only imagine the pain this irony must have caused the fire's victims.

Nevertheless, the residents of the hamlet soon came together to rebuild the necessities of Snyderville. Reportedly within a week's time, Joseph Beck had the frame of his new grocery already underway. The Fischer family, who lost virtually everything in the fire, reestablished their saloon in a small frame structure east of the Becks' new construction. Requiring a larger area to

Having lost their original store in the fire of 1905, the Fischers relocated their store into the post office building until their reconstruction was complete.

relocate their two-story general store, however, the Snyders offered them use of the post office building. Erecting a sign reading "Fischer Bros: Groceries, Flour, Feed and Etc.," the Fischers and Snyders worked together in this cramped building for nearly a year. Their cooperation and friendship is just an example of how close the ties of this community must have been.

As the rest of the community rebuilt, the Kabel family suffered another tragedy the following year. According to the *Amherst Bee* dated December 6, 1906:

> *Snyder had another big fire when the large barn on the property of John Kabel, on the south side of the Main Road, was burned to the ground. Fourteen cows, two horses and seven pigs were burned to death. The Kabel family was at their summer home when the fire broke out. Help arrived first with the Williamsville Hose Co. as the street car company ran a car carrying firemen and a flat car carrying the hose cart. Shortly after, a hose cart arrived from Buffalo.*

THE SNYDER HOSE COMPANY

In the years that followed, the continued growth of the village, as well as the memory of the fire that destroyed more than 50 percent of its buildings, propelled the discussion of fire protection. When the Western New York Water Company placed water mains in the area, the Snyder townsfolk gathered in Fischer's Hall on Main Street and became part of history. The year was 1915, and records indicate that paperwork granting Snyder an Incorporated Hose Company was signed on November 26 and was quickly approved by the Amherst Town Board on December 6. The first official meeting of the new Snyderville Hose Company was held at the old schoolhouse on December 20, 1915, and plans were finalized for the establishment of a fire district. Twenty-three volunteers, including Solomon Snyder, immediately signed on for duty.

Knowing that every good fire department needs strong leadership, the men quickly elected Edward Weitz president of the first Snyder Hose Company and Edward Helfter as the first chief. Meetings were held in the

An original member of the Snyder Hose Company, Solomon Sherman Snyder's badge remains a prized possession for his descendants.

old schoolhouse during 1916 and 1917, and among early orders of business were fundraising and the purchase of equipment. To help raise funds, the hose company hosted a card party and dance on February 16, 1916. To help with equipment, Michael Fischer, a well-known Snyder businessmen and hose company director, announced that his business, Fischer Bros., would donate 250 feet of fire hose and a hose cart. Apparently, the donated hose cart was in poor condition, however, for at the department meeting on June 5, 1916, three men were appointed to meet with the fire commissioners and ask that they get the fire apparatus and hose in shape. Subsequently, the men engaged in a thorough overhauling and repair of the hose cart and apparatus. The site for this work, coincidentally, was in Helfter's wagon works, the origin of the great Snyder fire!

Later that year, ladders, axes and lanterns were also purchased to equip the cart. Upon completion, the hose cart was first stored in a barn located on firefighter Joseph Beck's property at Main Street and Harlem Road. In 1917, it was moved to a barn located on the Snyder estate, which was leased by firefighter Michael Fischer. In 1920, a garage was built at Main Street and Lincoln Road for the purpose of storing the cart. The garage was referred to as "the little red barn" and remained on the site until the fall of 1948. The department purchased its first turnout gear in 1918, when $89.03 was paid for fifteen used raincoats and twelve hats. In 1921, electricity was installed in the garage. As for protocol, in the event of a fire, a passing motorist would be stopped and the cart would be attached to their vehicle. When no vehicle was available, the firefighters would use a long rope and pull the cart to the scene of the emergency.

As an attempt at an alarm system, the group constructed a tripod near the rear of Helfter's barn. Mounted atop was a large iron ring. With a mate placed about one hundred yards from Main Street on Washington Highway, the iron ring alarms were struck with sledge hammers to alert the volunteers of a fire. Last but not least, the men also created the original Snyder Hose Company badge.

Once established as firefighters, the men held meetings in the loft of Robert Conn's barn on North Harlem Road. By 1919, however, Emil H. Bergens, president of the company, gained possession of the Snyder property located in the Main Street and Lincoln Road area and offered to sell a lot to the company. If the company decided to purchase the lot from him, he offered to donate an additional, larger lot adjoining the purchased property. Bergens, together with his business partner Mr. Adam Shabtac, turned the deed to the donated plot of land over to the hose company at the department meeting

Members gather at the corner of Main Street and Lincoln Road for the annual Snyder Hose Company picnic on August 24, 1924. *Courtesy of the Snyder Fire Department.*

on April 3, 1922. The extra four lots were to the rear of the original plot of land and were to be used for parkland and picnics. Ground was broken for the new station on Monday, March 20, 1922, and a team of horses and skids soon dug out the basement. A grand ceremony was held to celebrate the laying of the cornerstone on Sunday, May 14, 1922.

Soon after the erection of the new hall, a Ladies' Auxiliary was formed to help the company raise money. Together, the ladies hosted picnics, threw card parties and arranged entertainment activities for the people of the village. With its first endowment from the Ladies' Auxiliary, the Snyder Hose Company proudly purchased an Ahrens-Fox Fire Pumper. Snyder's first motorized fire engine was shipped to the department on July 20, 1925, and served the department proudly for many years. By 1927, the hose company was in full swing and the *Audubon Topics*, a community newspaper, reported in its March edition the proper procedure for residents to follow to report a fire: "Use phone. Tell operator you want to report a fire to the Snyder Hose Company. She will then connect you with Beck's Meat Market. Give him the location of the fire. This applies day and night. Should operator fail to get Beck's Meats, she will attempt to notify several other members listed."

With help from the new Ladies' Auxiliary, the Snyder Hose Company purchased the Ahrens-Fox Fire Pumper in 1925.

As the years progressed, the company valiantly remained up to date in its equipment and tactics. Triumphantly, the Snyder Fire Department had the distinction of being the first 100 percent radio-equipped municipal volunteer fire company in Western New York. The technology allowed the placement of a receiver on each piece of firefighting equipment as well as in the home of each volunteer. This was certainly a far cry from a company that started with a hose cart, two iron rings and a sledgehammer.

After seventy-four years of service, the original brick fire hall at 4531 Main Street was destroyed in the spring of 1996. According to fire department historian and current chief Thomas A. Merrill, "An emotional farewell party was held at the old station on February 17, 1996, and on February 28, 1996, after a series of moves, all operations commenced from Chateau Terrace. In March, members gathered to watch the wrecker's ball demolish seventy-four years of history as the venerable old edifice came tumbling down. Construction of the new station had begun!"

Unfortunately, during the construction of this new building, a costly burglary took place. According to Amherst Police, an unknown number of perpetrators dismantled a plywood panel that covered the rear unfinished door and forced their way into the building. The burglars then removed $7,500 in oak trim and $2,500 in tools without being noticed by local

Snyder firefighters battle a blaze at 4543 Main Street on January 15, 1956. *Courtesy of the Snyder Fire Department.*

In 1925, Snyder firefighters included Louis Ball, William Sanford, Louis Wannenwetsch, Erven Doan, Howard Foell, George Baer, Leo Burgoyne, Albert Wolfe, Otto Beck and Joseph Schaetzer. *Courtesy of the Snyder Fire Department.*

residents. The theft was not discovered until the workmen arrived the following morning.

At completion, the community had erected an extensive Snyder Fire Department complex that, among other things, provided direct Main Street access to the emergency vehicles. All apparatus was moved into the new facility on the evening of Wednesday, January 15, 1997, and a new era of Snyder firefighting had begun.

In the decade since, the Snyder Fire Department has continued to live up to the high standard set for it. From the original twenty-three men in a barn to a present crew of seventy plus who respond to twelve hundred calls a year, the Snyder volunteers have never faltered in their dedication or their ideals. In 1997, Thomas Merrill said it best:

> *Through the years and all the changes, one thing has remained constant. Men and women from all walks of life have continued to step forward and volunteer. They have bonded together with the single concept of service to the community. As we approach the new century, Snyder residents may rest assured that no matter what the emergency, the thoroughly trained and dedicated members of the Snyder Fire Department will be there in time of need.*

CHAPTER SEVEN

DEVELOPMENT

A Surge of Housing and Growth of Neighborhoods

As previously stated, the advent of the Toonerville Trolley was paramount in the maturity of the Snyder area. In addition to the elite Buffalo families who chose to relocate and build sprawling Snyder estates, easy access to new housing developments also made it possible for the middle class to seek a Snyder home. Early farming families found it advantageous to sell their acreage to builders who envisioned Snyder in a new way—as a suburb. Thus, the change began to take place that led residents off the farm and into something new: a neighborhood.

COLLEGE HILL

In 1911, two brothers by the names of Arthur and William Suor had a vision. Although originally in the business of buying and selling traditional farm homes, the team was able to take this experience and create a new generation for real estate sales in Snyder: they invented a suburb. Purchasing ninety-nine acres of the Kabel family's farm, the brothers envisioned a neighborhood development project to be known as Amherst Heights. Working on the south side of Main Street between Getzville and Harlem Roads, the brothers began to carve streets and designate neighborhoods, using Washington Highway as the central point. Wishing to remain close to the project, Arthur took up residence in the Kabel family's brick farmhouse, located on Main Street just a little east of Washington Highway. By 1912,

Suor and Suor's College Hill sales office, located at the southwest corner of Main Street and Washington Highway. *From the collection of Amherst Museum, Amherst, New York.*

Currently operated by Hunt, the sign at 4363 Main Street proudly reminds customers of their service "since 1911."

William had finished construction of his own house on the eastern corner of the same street. Although Arthur's home has long since been gone, William's home still proudly stands as 6 Washington Highway.

For the next several years, the team developed middle class–size homes on Washington Highway and the surrounding streets and renamed their project College Hill. College Hill homes were mostly of two stories, boasted four bedrooms and included a den. Most importantly, these homes had the luxury of maintaining a bathroom on each floor. By 1919, the team of Suor and Suor had pulled together a deal to purchase an additional sixty-five acres of Tobias Witmer's farm, which was located to the south of their development and extended toward Kensington Avenue. Here, the team used larger lots to build more upscale homes and plan for more elaborate landscaping and street furniture. Christening this 331-lot parcel College Hill Terrace, the Suor brothers began to work their way toward the then underdeveloped Kensington Avenue region.

Looking down Washington Highway toward Main Street, the College Hill development begins to take shape. William Suor's house stands on the corner. *From the collection of Amherst Museum, Amherst, New York.*

Piggybacking on their residential success, the brothers sought out the Kensington Avenue area for commercial development. As reported by the *Amherst Bee* in June 1931, "The Suor and Suor Building Co. of Snyder is drawing material in preparation for the construction of stores at the corner of Kensington and Harlem." For the first time, businesses could be brought off the Main Street thoroughfare and capitalize on a different pathway to the Buffalo area. By the 1932 publication of Amherst High School's yearbook *The Tower*, the Red & White Stores advertised from their location at Harlem and Kensington: "Quality or Price: It makes no difference which, for you get both." Their neighbor, Shupe Co. Dry Cleaning, claimed "10% off for Cash and Carry." Stewart's Delicatessen at 458 Harlem Road near Kensington also advertised:

> *If you are planning to entertain your friends at luncheon, or if you want to treat your family to an appetizing meal, you may be sure your efforts will be successful if you buy your supplies at our store. High grade goods at low prices. For dessert buy Fro-Joy Ice Cream. We carry a line of school supplies, smokers' supplies, candies, sodas and other articles too numerous to mention. It will pay you to visit our store.*

Herzel's Drug Store at Harlem and Kensington also chipped in with an ad proclaiming itself as "The Home of Smacking Good Sodas—Where Courteous Service Reflects Appreciation—You Telephone, We Deliver." Oddly enough, the ad did not contain the store's phone number. Finally, Heiser's Dry Goods Store, also at Harlem and Kensington, boasted "Notions, Art Goods, Novelties—Furnishings for the Entire Family." Its phone number of "Crescent 2563-W" was included.

Whether working on commercial or residential affairs, the Suor and Suor headquarters thrived out of a humble real estate office on the southwest corner of Main Street and Washington Highway. Presenting a street sign that claimed "College Hill—A Good Place to Live," the small office embodied the quaint and homey atmosphere of the growing neighborhood. Maintaining its original integrity, the office, now part of Hunt Realty, still stands today, seemingly identical to the day it was conceived.

AUDUBON TERRACE

Working to the east of Suor and Suor, Charles Burkhardt embarked on the creation of the Audubon Terrace development. Beginning his work on the north side of Main Street, Burkhardt created a string of brick homes, all built in similar style. Just east of Burroughs Drive, the stately homes boasted large front yards, a modest amount of rooms and easy access to the trolley line. Purchasing more acreage adjacent to Audubon Terrace, Burkhardt created Audubon Heights and Audubon Park to entice the eyes of more wealthy home buyers. The development's headquarters was located in a white home on the southeast corner of Main Street and Darwin Drive, still standing today.

Moving to the west of his original Main Street projects, Burkhardt began to flesh out artistically designed streets both to the north and south of Main Street. He planned for homes on lots that would range from 50 to 90 feet wide and 160 to 300 feet deep. Employing a small selection of different builders, the development soon filled with homes of various styles and price ranges. Originally beginning with Burroughs Drive, Burbank Drive and Smallwood Drive on the north and Lamarck Drive, Huxley Drive, Walton Drive and Darwin Drive on the south, the Audubon district was beginning to take shape.

In an effort to attract customers to Snyder, Burkhardt published a sales packet detailing the Audubon Terrace project. According to Burkhardt's team:

This view of Lamarck Drive under construction shows several interesting points which illustrates the permanence of improvements at Audubon Terrace.
(1) Manhole, showing depth of pavement in the center of the street.   (2) Curbs, showing depth of pavement at sides.   (3) Water valve.   (4) Storm water outlets.

This excerpt from Charles Burkhardt's advertising brochure for the Audubon Terrace development shows the construction of Lamarck Drive. *Courtesy of the Snyder Fire Department.*

Close to every large city, yet distinctly apart from it, you will find one suburban residential district that is pre-eminently the finest. This suburb becomes the home of the city's discriminating families…For two miles and a quarter north from the city line, Main Street climbs a gentle slope. On the crest of this elevation lies Audubon Terrace—660 feet above sea level, 87 feet above Lake Erie. The sweet fresh air, immediately noticeable, is the first indication of the country like charm to be enjoyed here.

With regard to his vision, Charles Burkhardt should be remembered for his attention to detail. Understanding that it was more than a house that enticed people to a neighborhood, his teams would pay special attention to the street furniture used in his developments. Wishing to give his neighborhoods the aura of grand estates, Audubon Terrace employed such street fixtures as stone walls, pavilions, gates, weather vanes and iron artistry as street entrances. It was also decided to name many of the streets after famous naturalists and incorporate their unique stories into the artistry of the street furniture. Darwin Drive, for example, features a stunning cut-metal street sign. Depicted on the sign is the silhouette of a scholar, presumably Charles Darwin, seated at a table with an inkwell, a skull and a snail. The entrance to Darwin Drive is set off by massive stone walls and pillars, each topped with elaborate light fixtures and connecting to a wrought-iron arch over the sidewalk. The entrance to Lamarck Drive is of similar significance, being constructed in corresponding fashion and employing cut-metal signs of Indian teepees and hunters carrying a slain deer on a stick. Across Main Street, Smallwood Drive is set off by a pair of elaborate stone pavilions with copper roofs. Each gazebo enshrines the sidewalk as neighbors gallantly pass into the Smallwood development.

According to the marketing materials, "Audubon Terrace is the essence of high character in real estate. Each street is laid out for beauty as well as utility." Not only concerned with the entrance aesthetics, Burkhardt also beautified his streets with unique and elaborate landscaping.

All parkways are laid out as 85 foot highways with two 20 foot roadways or a single 35 foot roadway paved with a macadam. Grass areas in the center or on the sides are planted with perennials, ever-greens, and flowering shrubs…Shade trees are planted at 40 foot intervals between the sidewalk and curb on both sides of the street and street lights are erected similar to those in Delaware Park.

A fine example of Charles Burkhardt's street furniture, this structure at the entrance to Lamarck Drive typifies the Audubon Terrace grandeur.

With the Audubon Terrace sales office located on the corner of Main Street and Darwin Drive, this impressive entrance structure was a solid selling point.

Streets such as Burroughs Drive and Burbank Drive eventually became noteworthy for the arch of trees that would come to grow over the street. Bentham Parkway and Roycroft Boulevard were adorned with central malls that ran through the middle of the street and gave the neighborhood a park-like atmosphere. Each of Burkhardt's neighborhoods was special, having its own unique and elegant details. As the years passed and his trees grew, all who traveled the Audubon district were struck by their beauty. In 2006, however, an October storm wrought insurmountable damage to much of the development's original landscaping. Despite protests from Burroughs Drive residents, in 2008, nearly half of the street's trees were slain after suffering extensive storm damage and being deemed unsalvageable. Unfortunately, this was the scene around many other parts of Snyder as well.

In the end, residents were able to move into Audubon Terrace with water, electricity and toll-free phone service already in place. Two major highways, Main Street and Kensington Avenue, led directly to Audubon Terrace, and Burkhardt was quick to point out that several new venues, to be called Saratoga Road, Kings Highway and Wehrle Drive, would also connect to it. In his own words, "In short, it is the most desirable place one can choose to live. It is the city's finest residential district."

CHATEAU TERRACE

Looking at the north side of Main Street, just west of Harlem Road, developers began to envision a hidden neighborhood that would reside several hundred feet behind Abraham Lincoln Snyder's Main Street house. The Chateau Terrace district would be a secluded neighborhood, with only one means of entrance. Thanks to the winding nature of the access road and some strategically placed trees, the neighborhood would not be visible from Main Street, providing residents with both privacy and easy access to the village outside. Constructing the development in a circle, Chateau Terrace maintained an outer and inner circle and presently consists of the main Chateau Terrace as well as south, east and north terraces. The rear of the development, North Chateau Terrace, bordered the grounds of the Park School of Buffalo, which added to the secluded and park-like nature of the neighborhood. By 1924, interested residents were buying plots and designing their own houses. Mostly middle-class in size, styles varied as to the homebuyer's taste and made for a variety of sizes and styles.

Pictured following the October storm, this house at the corner of Chateau Terrace and Chateau Terrace South was one of the first to be built.

One such homebuyer was Gustave A. Duerstein. From his Buffalo home at 546 Northampton Street, "Gus" Duerstein pored over plans for his new Chateau Terrace home. Having purchased "Lot 9" in 1925, Duerstein was in search of a suburban home for himself and his three grown daughters. On May 28, 1926, the family received an offer from Fred F. Rievert, who bid $9,700 for the finished product. After two years of futile negotiations with Rievert, Holler Brothers Builders of Kenmore ultimately won a deal with Gus. The contract called for a total of $7,622 and guaranteed completion by September 15, 1928. Considering that the contract was dated June 7 of the same year, the plan was more than acceptable. For a design, Gus chose "a house to be built similar to the one built by Holler Bros. at #209 Crosby Ave." Insisting on the finest quality building materials, the Duersteins' house spared no expense. Employing elaborate gumwood woodwork, the home featured a decorative mantelpiece, recessed cabinets in the living room and breakfast nook, ornate banisters and hardwood floors. By the end of the year, Gus and his daughters, Laura, Edna and Florence, moved into their new neighborhood. With the exception of Florence, the remainder of the

Duersteins lived in their masterpiece, now 74 Chateau Terrace, for the rest of their lives. In 1980, after fifty-three years in the Duerstein family, the house was auctioned off to settle the estate. Two generations of the subsequent family have remained there ever since.

CHARLES LANDEL, HOMEBUILDER

By the onset of the Depression, the Chateau Terrace district had begun to fill in. It was at this point that my maternal grandfather, Charles Landel, a Snyder homebuilder, began construction on the house next to the Duersteins. Living just a few streets away at 37 South Harlem Road (now 4344 Harlem Road) made for an easy commute for the builder. Originally from Williamsville, it is truly a fluke that the Landels came to reside in Snyder at all. According to Dorothy (Landel) Shaver (1916–   ), in the late 1920s, she, her father Charlie and mother Irene (1891–1976) were living in a Landel-built house on Smith Street (now California Drive) in Williamsville. Her father had already completed construction of the house on Harlem Road and had begun a house for his mother, Julianna Landel, on Oakgrove Drive. Having already sold the family farm, however, Julianna had nowhere

Builder Charles Landel's homestead at 4344 Harlem Road. Landel erected several houses in the Snyder and Williamsville area and served the Bank of Williamsville.

to go in the interim. Being a generous soul by nature, Charlie immediately lent the Harlem Road house to his mother and sister Cora. After their stay, he intended to sell the dwelling.

It was not until after his mother moved into the Harlem Road house that fate took an ironic turn. According to Dorothy, her father Charles returned home one day and, out of the blue, announced to the family that he had sold their house. Apparently, one of his clients had made him an offer he could not refuse. When Irene worriedly questioned him where the family would go, he confidently replied that they would retain ownership of the Harlem Road house. Unfortunately, if you recall, this house was currently occupied. Not a man to go back on either deal, Charlie and the Landels faced a most unusual problem for a house builder—they were homeless. Nevertheless, the Landel family packed their belongings and headed for Snyder. Unwilling to impose on Julianna and Cora, Charlie engaged in the quintessential display of a boy's love for his mother and settled his family in the garage.

Once situated, Dorothy recalls her mother putting up curtains in the tiny windows and carrying water back and forth from the house. The cooking was done on a small hot plate and heat was provided by a rugged wood-burning stove. Despite the many inconveniences, the most unfortunate part of this arrangement was that it lasted into the winter. In what must have seemed like an eternity, Charles finally finished his mother's house in the middle of December. In a most festive atmosphere, the Landel family assumed residence in the house now marked 4344 Harlem Road the week before Christmas 1924.

Finally in the house, the Landels accumulated over fifty years of happy memories, including the birth of their daughter (and my mother) Lois (Landel) Fiddler (1931–   ). Even after their girls were married and raising children of their own, Charlie and Irene remained true to this house. With the addition of a downstairs bedroom and bathroom, my grandparents lived on Harlem Road into their late eighties. The upstairs was converted to an apartment and rented to an elderly couple from their church. Following the death of her parents, Lois and her family shortly invaded the quiet house. Interestingly, even after the house was reestablished as a one-family home and the upstairs apartment was reclaimed for bedrooms, the Fiddlers still had to deal with the sink, cupboards and stove outlet in the closet of the master bedroom. Their bedroom, dressing area and walk-in closet were the old apartment's living room, eating area and kitchen. After living in the house for only a short time, the Fiddlers sold the house in the fall of 1980 and returned to Chateau Terrace. Upon a 2007 tour of the Landel house,

Landel family visitors to the master bedroom were delighted to see that the quirky remnants of the old apartment remain, forever telling the story of an era gone by.

Being firmly set up in his Harlem Road house, Charles continued construction on the various new developments of Snyder and Williamsville. Along with Charles Burkhardt, Charles Landel served on the board of directors for the Bank of Williamsville and financed many of his houses through it. Frugal and successful, Charles and his business remained secure through the stock market crash and the ensuing Depression. As many of his contemporaries were not so lucky, however, their combination of circumstances directly led to the development of the Chateau Terrace lot next to the Duersteins.

During the Depression, Ray and Ruth Hall owned 78 Chateau Terrace, which was just an empty lot. The couple, however, soon fell in love with a house that Charles Landel had just completed on Los Robles in Williamsville. In order to purchase this new house, the Halls gave the 78 Chateau lot to Charles as a down payment. At this point, Charles's daughter Dorothy recalls her father coming home with another unusual announcement. Reminding

Pictured following the Blizzard of 1977 are the Duerstein house at 74 and the Landel two-family house at 78 Chateau Terrace.

A past view of the west side of Main Street between Bernhardt Drive and Lincoln Road.

A present view of the west side of Main Street between Bernhardt Drive and Lincoln Road.

everyone that it was the Depression, he said that he had a plan to help some of his friends who were not faring as well as he. In an effort to "put his friends to work," Charles had decided that he was going to build a two-family house on the empty Chateau Terrace lot. Although he had no need for the finished product, he had decided to provide low-rent housing for local families who may not have had the resources to buy. Soon, with his mismatched troop of workers, the brown and white house was underway. Today, 78 Chateau Terrace, as well as some of its peculiarities, still stands as a living testament to Landel's efforts to combat the Depression. The tale of its creation also answers the plaguing question, "How come you always have to shave off the sides of the switch-plates to fit next to the door frame?" The answer: "Because the guy who put the electrical box in was probably an unemployed accountant."

After its completion, the first to rent the lower apartment was Reverend Stoll of Ascension Lutheran Church. At this time, the present church at Main Street and Burroughs Drive was not yet built and the congregation met for worship in the Snyder Fire Hall. It was to this Chateau Terrace house that the Reverend would someday bring his happy bride. Also living in this house was the Cummings family. Originally owning a large house on Darwin Drive, the Cummingses saw their fortune erased by the Depression and subsequently lived in this apartment until their deaths. Although Charles originally sold the property to his daughter Lois in the 1950s, it is presently her sister Dorothy who owns and resides in her father's community-built house.

CHAPTER EIGHT

EDUCATION

From One-Room Schoolhouses to Elite Public and Private Schools

SCHOOL DISTRICT #2

Following the Common School Law of 1812, a community school was created at Main Street and Burroughs Drive. Welcoming its first class in 1813, School District #2 served a population encompassing Snyder and the village of Williamsville. The first class had twenty-six pupils, and classes for them were held in the spring, summer and fall. During this time, school operated six days per week to allow for the winter months when the weather conditions made it impossible to hold class. Although weather and other such interferences could make school attendance unpredictable, it was hoped that by each year's end, students would have accumulated about 110 days in the classroom. Without generous funding to sustain all of the school's needs, it was agreed that the parents would donate wood each fall in order to heat the schoolroom. In an effort to be "fair" to all parents, these donations were expected to be proportional to the number of children each had in attendance. Serving the hamlet's large families, such as the Snyders and Fischers, the school was able to successfully maintain its expenses.

In 1840, however, tragedy struck when the entire school building was destroyed by fire. Reopening in a rudimentary structure in 1841, enrollment rose to ninety students and Tobias Whitmer, who maintained a local farm between Main Street and Kensington Avenue, had agreed to teach a 106-day term for a salary of twenty-four dollars per month. The following year, a bid was made to extend the schoolhouse property, and within three years, a new brick schoolhouse had been erected. To beautify the grounds, the

Positioned on Main Street near Burroughs Drive, the brick schoolhouse for District 18 was erected in the mid-1800s and operated until 1924.

school's new teacher, Christian Frick, donated and personally planted eighty trees. The resulting campus became Snyder's own District #18.

At the turn of the century, School District #18 operated from 9:00 a.m. to 3:00 p.m. and students were called to class via the large outside bell. The school did not have a formal lighting system and contained no plumbing. Water was brought to the school in pails by neighbors and students. One pail was used for washing and one was reserved for drinking. Heat was provided by a wood-burning stove, whose care and maintenance was the responsibility of the teacher. The classrooms hosted double desks and blackboards at the front and rear of the room. Students were responsible for buying their own books and their curriculum encompassed reading, writing, arithmetic, spelling, history and geography.

In 1924, District #18 proudly moved into a new and much larger campus on Harlem Road. In following years, the original school building became a temporary home for Christ the King Church, Ascension Lutheran Church and the Amherst Senior Center. Upon demolition, in 1975, the old school grounds were divided into parcels presently occupied by the Snyder-Eggertsville Library and Ascension Lutheran Church.

Harlem Road School

The Alma Mater:

Truth and wisdom we have found here
Amherst 18
Happiness and joy abound here
Amherst 18
Deep devotion now we pledge you
Ever shall we praise your name
With our honor we address you
Amherst 18

Built in 1924, the Harlem Road School bordered Lincoln Road on the north, Coolidge Drive on the south and Bernhardt Drive to the west. The design was chosen to be a traditional Tudor Revival–inspired school building. The imposing structure had brick exterior walls with stone trim at the windows and doors, water table, frieze and cornice. What gave the school its enduring character, however, was the large pair of oak doors that

In 1940, the fourth-grade class of Harlem Road School #18 posed on the front steps. Included is Lois Landel, second from right in second row.

welcomed visitors who walked the long front sidewalk and ascended the wide stone stairs. Always loyal to its history, the Harlem Road School children of the 1970s and 1980s paid homage to this fine institution in a school song that reminded them:

Many who have come before us through the old oak doors
Are building us a better country—a community where everyone can live in
peace and harmony
So cheer the students of the past
For like them too, our time here will not last
Adventures wait for us to find beyond the oak doors
The world is waiting for what we have to offer

Once inside, students had access to two floors of classrooms, a gymnasium, auditorium, music rooms, art center and a unique basement-level cafeteria. Former student Dorothy Landel Shaver recalls making the transition from the original schoolhouse to Harlem Road. Meeting at the old Main Street building, the schoolchildren were escorted by their teacher on a walk to see

The 1981 sixth-grade graduation ceremonies at Harlem Road Elementary. The following year would see the last sixth-grade class at the school.

their new site. The new state-of-the-art school served the elementary-age population of Snyder, but upon reaching the high school level, students prior to 1931 were expected to relocate to Williamsville or Buffalo.

After proudly serving the youth of the community for sixty years, Harlem Road School was closed in the 1980s in a district-wide downsizing effort. Presently serving as the Harlem Road Community Center, the old school still caters to its community and enjoys the daily echoes of children's laughter inside its narrow halls.

AMHERST CENTRAL HIGH SCHOOL

The Alma Mater:

Voices hymn thy valiant praises, hearts thy halls enshrine
May our loyalty unceasing, Amherst, e're be thine
'Neath your towers facing northward we shall always be
Ever faithful Alma Mater to thy memory
When we leave thy halls of learning, paths of life to stray
May your guidance never ending, light us on our way
'Neath thy towers facing northward we shall always be
Ever faithful Alma Mater to thy memory
—G. Murray '39

Prior to the opening of Amherst Central High School, students from Snyder and Eggertsville were enrolled in Williamsville, Bennett or Neumann High Schools on a tuition-paying basis. In 1928, however, when the Buffalo Board of Education refused to enroll any new suburban students and raised the tuition for those already attending from $60 to $200, a crisis ensued. Thus, on April 2, 1929, the school boards from Snyder #18 and Eggertsville #13 banded together to form the Central High School District #1, a unique collaboration, the likes of which New York State had never seen. With the help of the town of Amherst, state aid was secured for the pioneering new school and the search for the ideal location began. By July 12, an agreement had been made and the citizens approved the purchase of the twenty-acre Pomroy property, located on Main Street next to College Hill.

Under the guidance of Crooker, Carpenter and Skaer general contractors, excavation for Amherst's very own high school began in November 1929.

Workers and horses excavate the grounds for the future Amherst High School on Christmas Eve 1929. *Courtesy of the Amherst Alumni Foundation.*

Obviously unable to accommodate students for the 1929–30 school year, about sixty ninth-grade students were transplanted to School District #18 on Harlem Road. The overcrowded school did its best to meet the needs of all of the students and all watched eagerly on February 22, 1930, as the cornerstone was laid and a new principal was hired.

Phillip A. Schweickhard came to Amherst with twenty years of school experience in Minnesota and a lifetime's worth of ideas and ideals. Beginning his tenure on July 1, Principal Schweickhard set up office in the only finished room in the building. From this third-floor classroom, he not only hired teachers and established curriculum but also purchased paint, furniture, equipment and supplies. Additionally, upon his arrival, one of the first matters attended to by the new principal was to remove markers that stated "Boys Entrance" and "Girls Entrance." Schweickhard envisioned an integrated school that students would be free to enter through whichever doors they pleased. In following years, Mary Schweickhard Spooner (class of '36) wrote to the Amherst Alumni Foundation that her father was rarely

Photographed looking toward the corner of Main Street and Washington Highway, workers frame the pool and east wing of the school, March 23, 1930. *Courtesy of the Amherst Alumni Foundation.*

Photographed looking toward the corner of Main Street and Berryman Drive, workers frame the future auditorium and stage, April 25, 1930. *Courtesy of the Amherst Alumni Foundation,*

The frame for Amherst High School's distinguishing tower has been erected, June 23, 1930. *Courtesy of the Amherst Alumni Foundation.*

Workers hurry to complete the front courtyard and erect the flagpole in time for school to begin in September, August 23, 1930. *Courtesy of the Amherst Alumni Foundation.*

home during the summer of 1930, working as many as twenty hours a day. Although only eleven years old at the time, Mary recalled installing the combination locks on all of the lockers and recording the combination in two places, per the instructions of her father.

Amherst Central High School officially opened in September 1930. Even at ninety-two, Dorothy Landel Shaver, a ninth grader at the school's opening, vividly recalls having to maneuver through the workmen just to get into the building. Since the front courtyard and grounds were still under construction, she reports walking a wooden plank through the construction site that led students to the side entrance doors. The three-hundred-member student body was served by a faculty that consisted of eighteen individuals each making $1,200 a year. At this juncture, the school building contained twenty-five classrooms and consisted of the north (upstairs) gym, pool, main hall and auditorium. Although underway, construction of the side halls would not be complete until 1936. The student body consisted only of seventh through tenth graders, due to the eleventh- and twelfth-grade students choosing to finish their education in the high schools in which they began. Although there was only one school building, the students were divided into a junior and senior high set. The junior high school consisted of grades seven through nine and the senior high school consisted of grades ten through twelve.

So it was in June 1931 when Amherst Central High School published its first edition of *The Tower*. The six- by nine-inch paperback featured a drawing of the school's "tower" on its orange cover and consisted entirely of students' literary work. To introduce what would become a staple in Amherst School publications, *The Tower* was dedicated with the following:

> *Foreword*
> *Amherst Central High School has no graduating class this year, nor, as yet any juniors. Its students, however, have shown the ability and the enterprise to present this record of the best school work of the freshman and sophomores. It is to be hoped that it will set a standard of literacy attainment against the day when class annuals begin to appear with their distracting tendency to allow scrappy and often trivial "features" to crowd out everything which is truly representative of the daily work of the High School. Future "Annuals," we trust, will aim to embellish rather than submerge the best literary product of which the able students of Amherst Central High School are capable.*
> —Philip Schweickhard, Principal, 1931

When school began in September 1930, classes were held in the main section of the building, as the side wings were not yet finished. *Courtesy of the Amherst Alumni Foundation.*

In the gymnasium located above the pool, the girls' gym class of 1930 waited patiently to begin their exercises. Pictured is Dorothy Landel, third from left. *Courtesy of the Amherst Alumni Foundation.*

By 1932, the paperback *Tower* posted advertisements as well as pictures of the freshman class, Glee Club, French Club and Dramatic Club. Featured Snyder advertisers included Stewarts Delicatessen, Red & White Stores, Frank J. Luense—Custom Tailor, Herzels Drug Store, Bank of Snyder, Heiser's Dry Goods Store, Schuler Brothers General Merchandise, Lincoln Beauty Shop, Schuler's Bakery, A.C. Koepf Flower Shop, the Open Door Gift and Tea Shop, Grieser's Naborhood Shoppe (library, school supplies, candy and ice cream) and Shupe Co. Dry Cleaning. The edition also paid homage to the first ever "Freshman Class Day," including a picture of the students gathered around the flag pole, as well as student body president Carl Anderson's speech. In this foundational speech, Anderson speaks of being a member of Amherst's first graduating class:

> *We consider it an honor to be the first class to graduate from the Amherst Junior High School. During our two years at Amherst, we have striven to live up to the ideals of the school. We hope that we are setting a good example for the future Freshman classes that will follow. Most of us, although we perhaps have not achieved honors as scholars, have helped in winning a name for our school by participating in activities. At any rate we honestly and sincerely tried to do our very best.*
> —Carl Anderson, Freshman Class President, 1932

By 1933, *The Tower* expanded to eight by ten inches and boasted a green suede cover. This edition would be the first true yearbook to be produced by Amherst and included a literature section, humor section and individual pictures of its first graduating class. The foreword, which was written by the students, was very simple: "If, in the years to come, this first year book of Amherst High School, edited by the first senior class, succeeds in bringing back some of the joys and friendships of our high school days, it will have fulfilled its purpose." Without a doubt, it is safe to say that this humble publication has more than served its purpose.

The 1933 and 1934 yearbooks make it clear that sporting activities were already beginning to gain momentum at Amherst. The 1932–33 school year marked Amherst football's maiden season and the dedication of Amherst's own gridiron on October 8, 1932. The football season consisted of eight games against schools in and around Buffalo, and according to the yearbook, the boys enjoyed a "very commendable season." By the 1924 yearbook, a black, hard-cover volume entitled *Ye Tower*, the following was written of Amherst football: "Three years ago, Amherst, inexperienced and scorned by their opponents,

Amherst High School's library as it appeared to the school's first students in September 1930. *Courtesy of the Amherst Alumni Foundation.*

began to build the foundation for its future football teams. Since then, we have gradually won the respect of the more experienced teams."

Tragically, however, the 1933–34 football season also claimed the life of one of its sportsmen. According to the *Amherst Bee* of November 9, 1933, "Arthur D. Kreger, 18, an Amherst High School senior, died from injuries sustained in a varsity football game last Saturday." Classmates paid tribute to Kreger that spring, when the following appeared in *Ye Tower*:

> *We of the senior class, as we near the close of our high school career, wish to pay tribute to the memory of a former classmate, Art Kreger, who was held in very high esteem by everyone coming in contact with him. It might be said of Art that he put his heart and soul into everything he did. He was an all-around athlete, starring in Baseball, Basketball, and Football. He has set an example of sportsmanship and courage that future Amherstonians might do well to follow. We will always cherish him as a true sportsman and a real credit to our school.*

The cafeteria at Amherst High School looked much the same in 1930 as it does today. *Courtesy of the Amherst Alumni Foundation.*

In the years following, Amherst football has consistently remained a competitive and revered sport. By 2006, the Amherst gridiron was covered with high-grade artificial turf, surrounded by a state-of-the-art track and electrified by stadium lights. Presently, Amherst's Dimp Wagner Field is revered as one of the finest high school venues in the state and hosts myriad other school sports, including soccer, field hockey and lacrosse.

Although football was certainly one of Amherst's most popular sports, it was not the first to produce an undefeated season. In a proud note from the 1934 yearbook, the staff reports: "Amherst experienced a new sensation this year when it was treated to an undefeated golf team, the first in the history of the school." Joined by talented teams in basketball, swimming and tumbling, as well as cheerleaders of both genders, the Amherst Tigers began to establish themselves as a force in the realm of high school sports.

Such were the state of affairs when forty-nine seniors crossed the stage of the Amherst Central High School auditorium on June 23, 1933. On this day, these men and women took their places in history and went on to become

Funded by the Amherst Alumni Foundation, the Amherst High School's Stone Tigers were dedicated during homecoming festivities in September 2008.

the first alumni class of Amherst High. In 1954, Principal Schweickhard laid the groundwork "to keep the Amherst family together" when he appointed Arthur E. "Doc" Pankow to coordinate alumni relations. Following that, the Amherst alumni tackled many projects, including creating newsletters and coordinating reunions. The present Amherst Central Alumni Foundation was conceived and incorporated in June 1983 and has spearheaded projects such as replacing the legendary oak doors and flanking them with a pair of stone tigers.

In the years following Amherst's first graduates, the high school's enrollment would continue to grow, and by 1949, the student population reached 1,507. In the following few years, additions would be made to the school, including a new gym and a music wing. With the 1955 relocation of grades seven through nine into the new junior high school, the campus underwent remodeling of the labs and home economics rooms and an enlargement to the second-floor gym. In the 1970s, the auditorium was updated and a library extension was added to the second floor. Following the turn of the millennium, the back courtyard was eliminated and a two-story addition was erected. Throughout the changes, however, Amherst High School has maintained the integrity of its past. Beneath the towers

A finished view of the state-of-the-art high school taken in the winter of 1931. *Courtesy of the Amherst Alumni Foundation.*

and past the ivy-coated walls, four generations of Amherst students have passed through the oak doors and left stronger for it. Although the faces change and the history lessons get longer, one thing never seems to falter—Amherst High School students enter the world prepared, passionate and proud to be Tigers.

SMALLWOOD DRIVE ELEMENTARY AND AMHERST JUNIOR HIGH (MIDDLE) SCHOOL

To meet the needs of the growing district, two new schools were opened in the 1950s. In 1951, a second elementary school was opened on Smallwood Drive that would serve students residing on the north side of Main Street. Harlem Road Elementary retained possession of the students on the south. Following the closing of the Harlem Road School, Smallwood became the solitary elementary school in the Snyder area. Creating a tradition of being named Business First's number one elementary school in Western New York, Smallwood Drive consistently prepares the youth of Snyder with the best education and most qualified personnel found in the area. By the year 2000, Smallwood entered the new century as one of the most distinguished and elite elementary schools in New York State.

In 1955, Theodore Masterson laid the cornerstone for Amherst Central Junior High School. Located on Kings Highway, directly behind the high school and across the athletic fields, the new school served the growing population of seventh, eighth and ninth graders. Opening on September 6, 1955, the junior high enrollment reached 1,050 students its first year. As described at the official dedication on April 29, 1956, the new school's opening was not without obstacles:

> *Anticipation, excitement and curiosity were at a high pitch. For weeks, workmen and children worked around each other. The meeting place for some classes shifted almost daily. No clocks, no bells, no cafeteria, no homemaking, no industrial arts, no music room, no gymnasium—all contributed to the difficulty of running the school program. Eleven hundred "supervisors" did their best to speed construction, but we did not take complete possession of the building until early January.*

Once in full operation, the junior high became a place of distinction.

Excelling in education as well as extracurricular activities, Amherst Junior High was renowned for its vocal and instrumental music programs, "frosh" sports teams and its award-winning literary magazine *Ventures*.

By the early 1980s, the Amherst schools were in the midst of change. Snyder's Harlem Road Elementary and Eggertsville's Eggert Road Elementary were slated to be closed and plans began to shift the grade levels in each school. In the fall of 1982, the sixth-grade classes were removed from the elementary schools and moved into the junior high. Spending two years housing sixth through ninth grades, the plan was in place to move the ninth grade to the high school, officially turning Amherst Junior High School into Amherst Middle. In the 1984 yearbook *Polaris*, Principal Anton Schwarzmueller speaks of this monumental change:

> *This unique and very special yearbook is a memento of a unique and very special year at A.C.J.H.S. Our second year as a 6–9 school is also our last year as a school that serves 9th graders. More than half of our students and a number of faculty members leave this June to become part of the new Amherst Senior High School next September while those who remain await the new Amherst Middle School.*

As a proud student of the final freshman class at Amherst Junior High, the author watched firsthand as the district suffered the loss of such things as frosh sports and Mrs. Sue Faye Allen's award-winning ninth-grade choir. The ensuing trip to the high school, however, proved that with every page turned, new adventures await. Presently, Amherst Middle School enjoys myriad modified sports and has welcomed the addition of a school musical every spring. *Ventures* literary magazine lives on and the music and art programs remain top-notch. If only the school could field a cheerleading squad again, all would be right with the world. Oh yeah…the education is still darn good too!

THE PARK SCHOOL

Opening in 1912, the Park School was founded by a group of parents who were committed to excellence in education and envisioned an atmosphere that encouraged students to discover their own talents in a unique setting. The group consulted with educational mastermind John Dewey and subsequently observed one of his students, Mary Hammett Lewis, at

Columbia University. Knowing that they had discovered a perfect fit, Miss Lewis was invited to Buffalo and became the founding headmistress of the unique school. Being both impressed and inspired by her experiences at this new school, Headmistress Lewis later wrote a book entitled *An Adventure with Children*. In the well-received volume, Lewis described her experiences at the Park School and how her children learned more than just schoolwork in this new and unique environment.

With Headmistress Lewis in place, the Park School, named for its proximity to Delaware Park, opened its doors to 27 pupils in the fall of 1912. Originally housed on Bird Avenue near the west side, the campus relocated to Main Street and Jewett Parkway the following year when enrollment skyrocketed to 100 pupils. By 1920, there were 127 students, with boys attending through sixth grade and girls through eighth. It was decided that the school's continued success would necessitate an even larger campus, and the search for the ideal location began.

Finding a perfect one hundred acres in suburban Snyder, the school arranged for the purchase of the Chauncey Hamlin estate on North Harlem Road. The Snyder estate boasted a spacious residence, farmhouse, barn, orchard and pond. Most notably, the purchase included the original Schenck stone house, which was perched at the Harlem Road entrance. Soon after purchase, the historic stone house endured a little remodeling in preparation for its use as the headmistress's house. In order to make the dwelling more comfortable, a fireplace was added to the living room and two dormer windows were added to the upstairs bedroom.

When the Park School opened its Snyder campus, classes for the older students were held in the Hamlin home and farmhouse and construction of the accommodations for the younger children was started. The younger children were treated to three enclosed bungalows, which were amply furnished with casement windows in an effort to bring the outdoors in. Even today, the concept of the school as "a little village" remains essential to the understanding and implementation of the Park School philosophy.

By the onset of the Depression, large chunks of the original one hundred acres had been sold in an effort to meet expenses. Enrollment, however, continued to grow, and a total of thirteen buildings were in operation on the thirty-two remaining acres. Having survived a few fires, including one large blaze in the early 1960s, the Park School presently serves grades pre-k though twelve and enrollment remains strong. Its students come from over thirty communities in the Buffalo-Niagara region, as well as from numerous countries and socioeconomic, racial, ethnic and religious backgrounds.

According to the school, "Growing up in such a diverse community is itself an invaluable element of a Park education."

Daemen (Rosary Hill) College

The Sisters of St. Francis of Penance and Christian Charity had been successfully operating D'Youville College, located on Buffalo's west side, since 1908. Wishing to expand and create a suburban women's college, the team, headed by Magdalene Daemen, began to look at Snyder real estate in 1947. Choosing a location on Main Street across from the Amherst High School, the sisters soon acquired land from the Mueller and Waite families. Most significantly, however, the future campus would also gain possession of the Renaissance-style Coplon and Gardner/Carson mansions.

Perfectly nestled on the corner of Main Street and Getzville Road, the new campus, named Rosary Hill College, due in part to its proximity to the College Hill development, received a state charter on July 31, 1947. Conceived as an arts and science college for women, the school began accepting enrollments in September 1947 but did not officially open until September of the following year, when forty-two freshman women became the first official class at Rosary Hill College. On hand to greet them were ten faculty members, including one priest, six sisters and three instructors.

Upon its opening in 1948, Rosary Hill operated entirely out of the old Carson mansion. Within its walls, students would find classrooms, a library, art studios, a bookstore, a cafeteria and faculty and administrative offices. Students were offered a curriculum based on the principles of general education, and this was followed by seven majors from which to choose. Being very well received, the curriculum served 158 students by the fall of 1951 and the faculty had expanded to include 29 personnel.

As growth continued, a separate classroom building, student center, science building, library and dormitories were constructed. A portion of the Campus Manor Apartment complex was also purchased as another option for student housing. The old Coplon mansion was named Curtis Hall and converted into office space, while the side apartment was utilized by the maintenance crew. Presently hosting faculty offices as well as the honors program, the outward appearance of the original Coplon estate has remained unchanged throughout the transition and is immaculately maintained by the college. Likewise, the Gardner/Carson mansion, now called Rosary Hall, remains as a showpiece of early twentieth-century

As the first male graduate of Rosary Hill College, James McNeill, pictured with his new wife Kathleen, received a bachelor's degree in theatre arts. *Courtesy of Jim and Kathy McNeill.*

architecture. Used as housing for the Sisters of St. Francis during campus expansion, Rosary Hall underwent extensive renovations near the end of the century. Rededicated on August 31, 1998, Rosary Hall, now the focal point of the campus, again became a center of activity, housing the offices of the vice-president of external relations, the director of alumni affairs, the director of the annual fund, the dean of enrollment management and admissions department staff.

As the years passed, Rosary Hill College made the decision to accept males in 1971. As the first male student, James McNeill became what he would describe as an "unintentional celebrity." Featured in newspaper articles and asked for pictures, McNeill received the first bachelor's degree awarded to a male in the school's history. He also has the distinction of being the first Rosary Hill graduate to receive the college's bachelor of fine arts degree in theatre arts. Although McNeill admits to working very hard for his degree, he wouldn't change a thing about his experiences. Often serving as director and head of set construction as well as an actor, the lone male learned valuable lessons in organization and time management. He also reports never being "distracted" by his female counterparts, having met his future wife, Kathleen Moore-McNeill, before enrolling at Rosary Hill. Purchasing a house on Chateau Terrace, the McNeills became permanent fixtures of the Snyder landscape. In the years following, Mr. McNeill would use his education to benefit the youth of Amherst, joining the faculty of the Amherst Central School District. Teaching at Eggert Road and Windemere Boulevard Elementary Schools, "Mr. Mc" raised five Amherst graduates of his own and remained a student favorite until his retirement.

Now coeducational, it was decided that Rosary Hill College would become an independent nondenominational college in 1976. Wishing to pay homage to its roots while still embracing the future, the name Daemen College was selected for this new venture, in honor of founder Magdalene Daemen. Presently, 2,300 students from across the United States and Canada come to Snyder and attend Deamen College. Seamlessly fitting into this tiny community, the students of Daemen enjoy their quaint campus as much as completing their homework at the nearby Denny's Restaurant.

CHAPTER NINE

RELIGION

A Diverse Community and Interdenominational Ideals

SNYDER'S FIRST CHURCH

Tandem to the growth and diversity of the new Snyder population was the growth and diversity of its religious beliefs. Although the early pioneers were predominately Mennonites who attended the Mennonite Meeting House on Main Street in Williamsville, the ensuing flux of residents came to Snyder with various religious affiliations. Finding a way to worship together, therefore, would necessitate some creative and, at times, groundbreaking ideas by the people of Snyder.

Snyderville's first church was located in the vicinity of the present HSBC Bank on the southwest corner of Main Street and Harlem Road. Previously established as a meetinghouse, religious services were held here on a weekly basis. Although the house and property were officially owned by John and Susan Frick, it was lent to the community free of charge. Adult religious services were held in the Fricks' meetinghouse every week. The children's Sunday school classes carried on in different homes in the area on a volunteer basis. Of equal importance, singing school was also hosted by a different family every Thursday evening.

AMHERST COMMUNITY CHURCH

By the early 1900s, as the community was truly starting to grow and diversify, citizens began to plan for a new Protestant church that would help to unify

The original Amherst Community Church was built on Washington Highway in the College Hill Development in 1916. *From the collection of Amherst Museum, Amherst, New York.*

the developing community. At this time, no such interdenominational churches existed in the greater Amherst area and the undertaking was a true pioneer effort. Finding many volunteers up for the challenge, however, Amherst Community Church was born in 1915.

At the inception, Baptist minister Robert M. Raab sponsored a series of meetings held in prominent community members' homes, such as Albert Homberger. Episcopalian Chauncey Hamlin, Methodist Arthur Suor, the Presbyterian Montgomery family and the Lutheran Avery family helped to complete the diversified group. Preachers from Buffalo and Williamsville donated their time to preside over many of the early services and the early members worked to set up a children's Sunday school. Also created was a women's society, whose initial purpose was to sponsor community-based fundraising activities and, subsequently, create a building fund. Among the proponents of a new building was business tycoon William H. Crosby, from just over the Eggertsville border. Originally a member of the Congregational church, Crosby donated both time and money to get this Snyder-based church off the ground. At that time, the board of trustees also consisted of Buffalo coal mogul Arthur Hedstrom, local business owner John Schenck and Snyder developer Arthur Suor. It was at this juncture that Arthur and his brother William Suor chose to donate a parcel of their College Hill development to the new church. Located on the west side of Washington Highway, the site was only a few hundred yards behind the College Hill rental office and a comfortable walking distance from most of the trustees' homes.

Hence, by 1916, Reverend R. Carl Stroll was hired as the congregation's first full-time pastor in the newly constructed Amherst Community Church building. Fundraising continued and on January 21, 1932, the *Amherst Bee* reported the following: "A gala party is planned by the Women's Association of Amherst Community Church for Friday evening, February 5, at 8 o'clock. It will be a hard time, old-fashioned costume party with entertainment, dancing, cards, grand march, Virginia reel and stunts. Admission will be 50 cents for adults and 35 cents for children."

Money raised though events like these funded later additions that included the current sanctuary, which was erected in 1951, and a major expansion and renovation in 1965, which added classroom space and a new library. A true pioneer in establishing a successful interdenominational church, the Amherst Community Church became part of the United Church of Christ at the time the denomination was formed in 1957. In 1985, the congregation chose to also affiliate with the Christian Church (Disciples of Christ) and the dual affiliation continues to this day.

As for the founding members, Amherst Community Church continued to be an integral part of their lives and identity. As noted in the *Amherst Bee* of August 9, 1956: "Funeral services for Mrs. Ida Heeb Suor, 81, of Snyder, were conducted on Saturday afternoon. Mrs. Suor died Aug. 2, 1956 at the Deaconess Hospital. Mrs. Suor and her husband, Arthur M. Suor, were among four families which founded the Amherst Community Church."

Thus, it is as a living testimony to the Suors, Crosbys, Schencks and Hedstroms that the Amherst Community Church thrives today. With the advent of a child care center and its use as substation for the Amherst Central School District's Universal Pre-K program, the church and the ideals on which it was built continue to be used every day, each doing their part to keep Snyder's community enlightened and fulfilled.

CHRIST THE KING ROMAN CATHOLIC CHURCH

During the time in which the Amherst Community Church sought to unionize the religions of the area, the Roman Catholic Church was also establishing a dominating presence of its own. Previously frequenting St. Peter and Paul Church in Williamsville, the people of the Snyder area were treated to news of their own parish on May 8, 1926. On that date, Most Reverend William Turner, then bishop of Buffalo, appointed Reverend Henry A. Mooney pastor for a new parish to be constructed in the rapidly expanding village of Snyder. Until a new church could be built, Mass was celebrated at the old Amherst District #18 school building, which was located on Main Street and Burroughs Drive. The new church was to be dedicated to Christ the King and had the honor of being the first in the world to bear that name.

While searching for the land on which to construct their new church, Charles Burkhardt, the Audubon Terrace developer, offered as a gift to the diocese a tract of land bordered by Kensington Avenue, Walton Drive and Huxley Drive. Father Mooney declined this offer, however, and instead requested the present Main Street location, bordering Lamarck Drive and Bentham Terrace. On this site, he wished to construct not only the church but also the pastor's residence, school and convent.

Accepting Father Mooney's plans, the cornerstone for the new construction was appropriately laid on October 27, 1928, the Feast of Christ the King. As construction commenced, community support increased and donations flooded in from excited Catholics. The stained-glass windows above the altar, depicting Christ the King and Two Adoring Angels, were donated by John J. and Esther Christ Horan. The facilities themselves were built in the form of an L, and the church was designed to seat about six hundred people. The section parallel to Main Street was to contain the school facilities on the first floor and the pastor's residence on the second floor. The basement included a parish club or meeting room, a kitchen and a bowling alley.

By the following year, construction was complete and on the 1929 Feast of Christ the King, Bishop William Turner offered the first Mass in the new Christ the King Church. In the days following the celebrated opening, however, the people of Snyder and the world at large would watch helplessly as one of the darkest days in the history of the United States began to unfold: the stock market crash of 1929. Bringing hard times upon the new church, the Depression encouraged the people of the parish to work together. Holding a number of fundraising activities to benefit the church, the people participated in activities such as card parties, dances, lawn fêtes, carnivals and the sale of fresh fruits and Christmas trees. For the sporting enthusiasts, there was even "prize fighting" that took place in a boxing ring set up in the church basement. Incidentally, one of the fighters who participated in this event was none other than Jimmy Goodrich, a well-known boxing champ of the 1920s.

The end of the Great Depression brought a renewed affluence to Snyder, along with an increase in population. In order to serve the growing community,

Ascension Lutheran Church/Crossroads stands at the corner of Main Street and Burroughs Drive near the site of the former School #18.

additional land was purchased and the present Christ the King School was built in 1952. A new rectory was completed in 1954 and an addition to the school was built in 1956. This addition included nine classrooms, a library, a nurse's office and a recreation center, which was named Mooney Hall after the first pastor, Reverend Henry A. Mooney. Also included in the 1956 construction was the installation of the marble statues of Christ the King and the Immaculate Conception, as well as new Stations of the Cross.

ASCENSION LUTHERAN CHURCH

With a growing number of Lutherans in the Snyder area, the idea arose to build their own Snyder-based church. Up until this time, many of Snyder's population attended St. Paul's Eggertsville or its sister church, St. Paul's Williamsville. Under the care of Reverend Stoll, a new congregation arose, and it was to be called Ascension Lutheran Church. Although homeless upon its creation, the people of the new church happily met for worship in the Snyder Fire Hall or the old School #18 building while they awaited their new facility. Securing a nearby lot at the corner of Main Street and Burroughs Drive, the present Ascension Lutheran Church building opened its doors in 1957. This beautiful brick church encompassed a traditionally quaint worship sanctuary, several Sunday school rooms, a meeting hall and a fully functioning kitchen. Soon, Garden Nursery School, one of the oldest and most revered nursery schools in Western New York, would take up residence on the lower floors. Presently offering a two-year-old program in addition to its traditional nursery school and four-year-old enrichment programs, the Garden of 2009 is still a place where the toddlers of the community can continue to grow.

In September 2007, a dwindling congregational base precipitated the combination of three area Lutheran churches: Ascension, Cleveland Hill and St. James. Beginning in January 2009, these three churches embarked on their own unique collaboration, combining traditional Sunday worship services with Saturday live jazz services and new Adult Education and Sunday school programs.

Still planning to utilize the original church at Main Street and Burroughs Drive, the people of Snyder once again embarked on a unique collaboration. By doing so, Snyder's present population continues to break new ground, proudly carrying on the traditions of the pioneers who first gathered here in an effort to worship together.

CHAPTER TEN

NATURAL DISASTERS

The Blizzard of 1977 and the October Storm of 2006

Located just south of Buffalo and in proximity to Lake Erie, Snyder and its residents have become accustomed to many variations of weather. In fact, if there is anything predictable about the weather in Snyder, it is its complete unpredictability. According to former Buffalo resident Mark Twain, "If you don't like the weather in Buffalo, wait five minutes." Yes, it may be seventy degrees on Christmas and it has been known to snow in May. Even for a place where residents have endured eight feet of snowfall in a single storm, hail the size of golf balls, a few mini-tornadoes, several ice storms and the traditional blizzard here and there, two events separate themselves from the ordinary. Their stories are legendary and their legacies live on in damage that may take a century to overcome.

THE BLIZZARD OF 1977

The inspiration for several full-length books, various quirky souvenirs and even a carefully planned board game, the blizzard that hit Buffalo and the surrounding areas in 1977 has become infamous. In total, twenty-nine people died during the storm that lasted from January 28 to February 1 and, thanks to President Jimmy Carter, became the first snowstorm to earn federal disaster area designation. Officially tallying $300 million worth of damages, the Blizzard of '77 remains a vital piece of local legend.

Meteorologically speaking, the combination of events that precipitated the great blizzard was truly unusual. According to the *Buffalo News*, "Lake Erie froze over by December 14, 1976, an early record. This normally puts an end to the lake effect snowstorms created by winds picking up moisture from the lake surface, converting it to snow and dumping it when those winds reach shore. But that winter something different happened."

Beginning after Christmas, snow fell virtually every day and began to bury Snyder and the surrounding regions at a steady pace. Nearing the end of January, almost thirty-six inches of snow blanketed the neighborhoods and three feet of snow rested atop the frozen waters of Lake Erie. According to residents, although the National Weather Service had issued a blizzard warning on the morning of Friday, January 28, the air outside was quite warm and calm. Although some schools closed in anticipation, many people ventured to work and carried on with their daily activities. By noon, however, conditions had quickly changed. As the temperature dropped to zero degrees Fahrenheit, winds quickly picked up. With gusts measuring over seventy miles per hour, the wind chill temperature plummeted to sixty degrees below zero. Although only seven new inches of snow would fall over the following days, the fury of the blizzard did not lie in the fresh snow but in the several feet that had accumulated on the ten thousand square feet of Lake Erie.

With the whiteout conditions and the severe drifting of blowing snow, it did not take long for residents to become stranded. By Friday afternoon, the Town of Amherst declared a state of emergency due to the poor visibility brought on from the swirling snow. An official reported to the National Weather Service that the visibility in Amherst was "absolutely zero." One local man, unable to continue driving in these conditions, attempted to ride out the storm in his vehicle. Amherst Police found him hours later, dead in his running car. An autopsy would confirm that the man died of carbon monoxide poisoning. Other victims, stranded in cars buried by snow, simply froze to death.

Over the next few days, blizzard-like conditions prevailed. According to the *Buffalo News*, "Here the wind was so strong that it broke up snow crystals and compressed them into drifts that were cement-like in quality. At the same time, buildings acted like snow fences causing the drifts to accumulate in some places to 30 feet, enough to bury a house."

As a result, thousands were stranded away from their homes and on January 28, for the first time in its 143-year history, the *Buffalo Courier Express* did not publish the morning paper. Although a driving ban had been in place since the beginning of the storm, by Sunday, January 29, several

Western New York communities had also banned snowmobiles, which had, until this point, been used as emergency vehicles. With the ability to ride on top of the ridiculously high drifts, snowmobile drivers volunteered to help the authorities by delivering medications and answering emergency calls. Unfortunately, incidents of snowmobilers being injured in collisions with roof chimneys and reports of others who had come dangerously close to hanging power lines necessitated the disbanding of the snowmobilers' volunteer army. Through it all, however, snow plow drivers still attempted to dig out their communities' streets. In his book *White Death: The Blizzard of '77*, Rossi tells the story of a rotary plow driver who was working in an area where snow drifts reached in excess of twelve feet high. "Asked if he was concerned about hitting buried objects, he said he wasn't worried about hitting a car, especially small cars. With a straight face, he said, 'Volkswagens are okay, they go through the rotary blades.'"

As difficult as the blizzard was for hospitals and fire stations, it also left funeral homes in a precarious position. While multiple deaths necessitated their services, the weather conditions often impeded their efforts. During the driving ban, Snyder funeral director Robert Fiddler would reportedly walk the two miles to Beach Tuyn Funeral Home on Main Street. Given the danger of venturing out during these few days, the funeral directors' loved ones became irritable, with one wife proclaiming, "They're already dead... they aren't going anywhere!" Regardless, funerals commenced, but burials were impossible due to the snow and frozen grounds. At Beach Tuyn, as well as most others, the caskets were stacked in the funeral home's garage, where they remained until spring, when the thaw finally made burial possible.

Storm-related deaths were also reported by the Buffalo Zoo. In total, over twenty animals perished during the blizzard, mostly water fowl and hoof animals that died of cold-related conditions. Two other deaths were wrought in conjunction with the case of three clever Scandinavian reindeer and two petting zoo sheep that simply walked up a snowdrift and over the outside fence. One of the reindeer died of shock after being chased by a snowmobiler in a Buffalo neighborhood and one of the sheep simply disappeared and was presumed killed by dogs. In the end, damage to the Buffalo Zoo was estimated at nearly half a million dollars.

For the people of Snyder, the ramifications of the blizzard also disrupted many facets of their everyday lives. With the region in shambles, a total of four Buffalo Braves NBA games and two Buffalo Sabres NHL games had to be postponed. Mail and newspaper delivery was also suspended for up to a week. Soon, reports of price gouging surfaced, with residents claiming to

On January 28, 1977, a blizzard of epic proportions buried Western New York. Pictured is the inner circle of Chateau Terrace after being plowed out.

have to pay seventy cents to a dollar for a sixty-cent gallon of gas. Others, unable to buy any gas at all, reported that stations were conserving their supply, only selling to "regular customers."

Over thirty years later, Snyder residents are still quick to tell you of their personal experiences during the great Blizzard of '77. Some recall hanging blankets over the windows to keep out the cold and the wind while others reminisce about forming neighborhood troops to check on the elderly. Reports of being trapped at the Eastern Hills Mall, Memorial Auditorium or a near stranger's house are not hard to come by. One Snyder gentleman, who was only eleven at the time, recalls his mother being trapped in Akron for several days. Working as a schoolteacher, she was released from the school early in the day but found herself trapped in her car on an Akron bridge. Heroically, one of her students found her, rescued her from the car and brought her to his home, where she remained until the storm had passed. It is this case and the thousands of others like it that encompass the spirit of Western New York at that time. Known as the "City of Good Neighbors," Buffalo and the surrounding suburbs certainly lived up to that name during the Blizzard of '77.

THE OCTOBER STORM OF 2006

Affectionately nicknamed such colorful monikers as the "October Surprise Storm," the "Friday the 13th Storm," the "Columbus Day Massacre," the "October Nightmare" and the all-encompassing "Arborgeddon," the storm that hit Buffalo and the surrounding regions on October 12–13, 2006, was one for the history books. Beginning as a rain and snow mixture in the afternoon of Thursday, October 12, as the temperatures quickly dropped, rain changed to ice. While snow began to accumulate on the ground, a slushy mixture clung to the brightly colored leaves, still hanging on the pretty fall trees. The addition of lightning and high winds created conditions unlike any seen before in the tiny hamlet of Snyder. According to the National Weather Service, what followed was an example of a unique and rare meteorological phenomenon known as "thundersnow."

Residents will not soon forget the haunting sounds that echoed through the air over the next several hours. As the thunderstorm continued and power lines fell, the full fall trees, unable to withstand the accumulation of ice and snow, split and crumbled beneath their own weight. While the winds whistled violently through the trees, continuous sounds of popping and crackling were intermittently followed by tremendous crashes as giant limbs and whole trees fell to the ground. As neighbors across the area ventured outside Thursday night to try and move their cars or clear the road, it became obvious that the danger of falling trees necessitated everyone to stay indoors. By 8:00 p.m., a transformer on Chateau Terrace was struck by a falling tree, causing an explosion on the utility pole. The sparks lit the backyard like the Fourth of July, but luckily, no fire ensued. Within hours, rooftops, parked cars and summer trampolines, not yet stored away for the season, were crushed under the enormous amounts of falling debris.

With virtually the entire town out of power, residents could do nothing Thursday night except try to keep safe and warm while the storm continued. With temperatures outside below freezing, many families slept together in one room to try and stay warm. Those lucky enough to have fireplaces huddled around them and hoped to have enough wood to ride out the storm. In the darkness, residents held their breath with each powerful gust of wind. During the early hours of Friday, October 13, almost worse than the cold and blackness were the sounds of breaking branches, large crashes and the fear of what the daylight would bring.

On the morning of Friday, October 13, the air was much calmer. The thunder had stopped and intervals between falling trees had widened. The outside air held the dense quiet so notable after a large snowfall, prompting

On the morning of October 13, 2006, streets were blocked by fallen trees and wires, and even walking your dog became a dangerous outing.

residents to peek out their windows and decide whether it was safe to venture outside. Upon surveillance, it was found that the fury of the storm had dumped a record-breaking thirty-six inches of snow on the Snyder area and the incomprehensible amount of damage here would later make the authorities deem it as the epicenter of the historic event. Amidst the danger of the falling trees, live wires canvassed the landscape, creating an obstacle course for anyone venturing outside.

At the height of the disaster, 90 percent of residents found themselves without heat and electricity. In the town of Amherst alone, nearly forty thousand residents found their houses dark, while the *Buffalo News* reported 397,000 outages for the region at large. By mid-morning, Governor George Pataki had declared a state disaster emergency. While cleanup orders were sent to the National Guard, a letter was sent to President George W. Bush asking for federal assistance.

Over the next several days, the area remained paralyzed by the storm. Non-emergency travel was forbidden and neighborhoods banded together to clear their own roads. As the town was still largely without electricity, the

Looking north down Smallwood Drive, residents dealt with toppled trees long after the original brush was cleared from the street.

sounds of generators hummed throughout the streets. Some residents, lucky enough to have their power restored, ran extension cords to surrounding houses, while others walked warm meals to neighbors without the use of their electric stoves. As the temperatures rose in the following days, those without power turned to their outdoor grills, not yet packed away for winter. Not only did the grilling provide a warm meal, it also enabled families to use the frozen meats that were sure to spoil without the benefit of a refrigerator.

The rising temperatures, however, initiated a second phase to the disaster already at hand—flooding. As the two feet of fresh snow began to melt, those without power began to experience flooding in their basements. As residents helplessly looked at their powerless sump pumps, many reported standing water up to their knees, with one resident experiencing a high of four feet. Although many families initially reported bailing water all night, efforts eventually switched to salvaging items when it became clear that the flooding was out of their hands. On Lakewood Drive, one family could do nothing but empty the entire contents of their basement's underwater rec room out onto the street.

As the days passed, more and more happy National Grid customers experienced the return of their electricity. Unfortunately, for many of the harder hit streets, several empty promises still left them without. Although the outer circle of Chateau Terrace had regained power just a few days after the storm, the inner circle, devastated by the explosion on the utility

A school bus attempts to maneuver down Chateau Terrace amidst the cleanup efforts that continued late into October.

pole, remained without nearly seven extra days. TV cameras and reporters from the *Buffalo News* circled the terrace and interviewed residents who had endured power outages longer than anyone else in the region. Finally, on October 23, the *Buffalo News* proudly ran the good news under the following headline: "Home stretch: Final neighborhood restored." For the first time in over ten days, Chateau Terrace electrified the night air and residents enjoyed their first night's sleep, unburdened by the loud humming of generators.

The schools in the Snyder area would also suffer major storm-related damage. In addition to the loss of trees, flooding ensued at Smallwood Drive Elementary and roof damage was reported at the middle school. Although most school districts in Western New York resumed classes on Monday, October 23, the Amherst School District remained closed until October 26 due to building damage and impassable roads. As the brush piles in front of houses were stacked in excess of eight feet tall and many sidewalks remained impassable from debris, children were escorted to school by parents and school personnel worked tirelessly to ensure the children's safety on the school grounds.

In the end, more than 90 percent of Snyder's trees were injured and virtually no household was immune from debris or flooding damage. As the school district scrambled to adjust its schedule to accommodate for the excessive snow days, residents began the journey back to a normal life. As Halloween approached and many roads and sidewalks remained covered in branches, many feared the neighborhood trick-or-treating may have to be cancelled. With the aid of out-of-state workers, FEMA and the National Guard, however, progress was made and the local ghosts and princesses were able to venture out into their tattered neighborhoods, forever scarred by the horrors from Friday, October 13, 2006.

A CHRONOLOGICAL HISTORY
OF SNYDER

1797 Abraham Snyder is born in Pennsylvania.

1804 Timothy Hopkins builds his house in Snyder and marries Nancy Kerr in the first recorded marriage in Erie County.

1813 School District #2 is formed. This would later become the Snyder School.

1821 John Schenck and family come to Snyder in a covered wagon. They settle near Main Street and Harlem Road.
Michael Snyder is born in Lancaster County, Pennsylvania.

1823 Abraham, Veronica and Michael Snyder leave Pennsylvania and travel to Snyder in a wagon train.

1832 Abraham Snyder boards an east-bound stagecoach and disappears.

1837 The Snyder homestead is built at the northeast corner of Main Street and Harlem Road.
Michael Snyder and John Schenck open a mercantile in front of the Snyder estates. The village of Snyder has begun.

1839 The Main Street Tollgate is established near Getzville Road.

1881 A fire erupts on Main Street near Freuhauf Drive. The Wittigs' property is destroyed, as well as the Freuhaufs' store.

1882 The Snyder Post Office is officially recognized by the U.S. government and Michael Snyder is named its first postmaster.

1892 The Buffalo-Williamsville Electric Railway is established. Locally, this was known as the Toonerville Trolley.

1901   Electric lights are installed on Main Street throughout Amherst.

1902   Michael Snyder dies at age eighty-three.

1905   Snyder burns violently. Twelve buildings are destroyed in a path spanning both sides of Main Street from Freuhauf Drive to Amherstdale Road.

1906   The Fischer brothers reopen their general store in a new two-story plank building.

1911   The Suor brothers begin construction of the College Hill development on Washington Highway.

1912   The Park School opens on Harlem Road, north of Main Street.

1916   Snyderville Hose Company is formed by twenty-three volunteers. Their equipment included one hose cart and two "iron ring" alarms.

1922   Tobias Witmer's farm is purchased by the Burkhardt Company, which begins construction of the Audubon Terrace district.
Snyder Fire Hall is established at Main Street and Lincoln Road.

1924   The Harlem Road School is completed and open to students. Presently, this building acts as the Harlem Road Community Center.

1929   Bank of Snyder opens at the southwest corner of Main Street and Harlem Road. This would eventually be converted to the HSBC Bank.
The great robbery of Snyder takes place at the Carson estate. Seven masked gunmen steal jewelry, furs and cash from party guests.
Christ the King Roman Catholic Church is dedicated at the corner of Main Street and Lamarck Drive.

1930   Amherst Central High School is opened to grades seven through twelve. The first registration totals 275 pupils and the first principal is Phillip Schweickhard.

1931   The Bakerts open their mom and pop store in the front of their house at 4209 Main Street. A legendary hangout for six decades of Amherst High School students, the Bakerts family operated this humble icon until 1985.

1947   Daemen College (aka Rosary Hill) opens across from Amherst High School and is marked 4380 Main Street.

1951   Smallwood Drive School opens.

1954   The western section of the New York State Thruway is completed. This new section is run through the limestone quarry once operated by the Fogelsonger family.

1955   The Snyder family house at the corner of Main Street and Harlem Road is destroyed.
Amherst Central Junior High School opens on Kings Highway.

1957   Beulah and Earl Fiddler move out of the original Abraham L. Snyder house at the corner of Main Street and Chateau Terrace and the Snyder branch of the United States Postal Office is erected in its place.

       Ascension Lutheran Church opens at the corner of Main Street and Burroughs Drive.

1958   The Schenck homestead at the corner of Main Street and Amherstdale Road is demolished. For well over one hundred years, this house stood on the property originally developed by Timothy Hopkins.

1961   The Eggertsville-Snyder branch of the Amherst Public Library opens on Main Street near Burroughs Drive.

1967   Scherer's Jewelry relocates the store it had operated on Fillmore Avenue since 1903. It assumes residence on the north side of Chateau Terrace. Eventually it would move across the street to the southeast corner of Bernhardt Drive.

1977   The Blizzard of '77 hits Buffalo and surrounding regions, paralyzing the area.

1989   Snyder's band hall/house is torn down. This was the last original Snyder family building.

1997   Snyder Fire Department opens its new and improved fire hall.

1998   Bornhava, a school for developmentally challenged preschoolers, opens in the vacant post office building at the corner of Main Street and Chateau Terrace.

2006   The October storm paralyzes the region for weeks and damages over 90 percent of the area's trees.

A WALKING TOUR OF THE
WILLIAMSVILLE CEMETERY

Owned by the Longs, the Williamsville Cemetery was originally a burial place for members of their Mennonite family. The oldest grave stone currently visible is dated February 2, 1810, although records indicate that it was not officially recognized as a burial ground until 1824, when it was opened up to the community. Since there is no official cemetery in Snyder, many of the hamlet's early residents were laid to rest in Williamsville.

For individuals like me, cemeteries are a curious and fascinating place. I believe that this plot of land is the closest I will ever come to being with a familiar friend or meeting an old-time legend face to face. Usually, I simply enjoy going to the cemetery to "visit." While I was researching the families of Snyder, I spent a great deal of time in this cemetery, gathering dates, spelling names and solving mysteries. Soon I found that each time I stood by Michael Snyder, Benjamin Long or Charles Landel, history was actually showing a movie in my head. It was almost as if I could watch many of the stories of this book unfold before my very eyes. When I stood on the Fogelsonger family plot, I saw their concert in Snyder's band hall when one of their musicians fell through the curtain and off the stage. Walking by Charles Fry, I could see him running full speed after the tollgate crasher. Finally, looking down at the grave of Veronica Snyder, I could feel the cold and empty spot next to her, kept vacant in honor of her husband who never returned. It was then that I conceived this idea of including a walking tour

Many of Snyder's early families were laid to rest in the Williamsville Cemetery. Shown here is the Snyder family section.

in this appendix. I have imagined it as a rendezvous for souls like me, who find the cemetery a place much more about life than about death.

Hence, the next time you find yourself on Main Street between Long and Reist, take a quick turn through the wrought-iron gates. Once inside, spend some time and introduce yourself to many of Snyder's interesting and unforgettable characters. You have already spent a fair amount of time peeking into their lives within the pages of this book; it's time they got the opportunity to peek into yours. If your imagination is anything like mine, it will be an experience you will never forget.

WHO'S WHO IN THE WILLIAMSVILLE CEMETERY?

Cemetery Section D (right front section)

Veronica (Schenck) Snyder — Wife of Abraham and mother of Michael and Jacob, Veronica traveled to Snyder from Stony Creek, Pennsylvania, in 1823.

Michael Snyder	The true father of Snyder, Michael lent his name to the village in which he lived. He is responsible for building the mercantile, band hall, courthouse, wagon works, blacksmith, cider mill, rug shop, post office and Snyder's Inn. Politically, he served as Amherst town supervisor, Amherst highway commissioner, Snyderville's justice of the peace and Snyderville postmaster.
Catherine (Halter) Snyder	Wife of Michael and mother to his eleven children.
Henry Snyder	Son of Michael and Catherine who died at seventeen years of age.
Edward Daniel Snyder	Son of Michael and Catherine and father to three "unclaimed" children.
Tobias Washington Snyder	Son of Michael and Catherine, Tobe served as Amherst town supervisor, as well as Snyder postmaster for twenty-two years.
Abraham Lincoln Snyder	The son of Michael and Catherine, Abe was named after his paternal grandfather. Marrying Grace Dryer and living at the corner of Main Street and Chateau Terrace, he worked as an auctioneer and had three children.
Grace (Dryer) Snyder	Second wife of Abraham Snyder and mother to his youngest daughter.
Solomon Sherman Snyder	Son of Michael and Catherine, husband of Caroline and father to Agnes, Beulah and Gladys, Solomon was a pioneer member of the Snyder Hose Company and lived in the old Snyder band hall.
Caroline (LeBrun) Snyder	Wife of Solomon and mother of Agnes, Beulah and Gladys, Caroline was a direct descendant of Charles LeBrun, first painter to King Louis XIV.
Charles Grant Snyder	Son of Michael and Catherine, Charlie was a bachelor who dabbled in horticulture.

Mary Snyder	Daughter of Michael and Catherine who eloped, only to be brought back home by her brothers on her wedding night.
Susan Snyder	Daughter of Michael and Catherine who died at birth.
Ida Snyder	Daughter of Michael and Catherine who died at five years of age.
Alta Snyder	Daughter of Michael and Catherine, Alta never married, but was famous for her sense of humor.
Florence Snyder	Daughter of Abraham Lincoln Snyder who was legally adopted by her grandparents, Michael and Catherine.
Arthur Snyder	Son of Abraham Lincoln Snyder who was legally adopted by his grandparents, Michael and Catherine.
Agnes (Snyder) Wannenwetch	Daughter of Solomon and Caroline, Agnes lived in the band hall house after her parents passed away.
Gladys (Snyder) Church	Daughter of Solomon and Caroline who was known to her friends as "Toodles," Gladys spent the Roaring Twenties touring the country with her troop of friends and relatives.

Cemetery Section B (left front section)

Jacob Snyder	Son of Abraham and Veronica Snyder and brother of Michael, Jake is fondly remembered as an entertaining character.
Fanny (Long) Snyder	Wife of Jacob and descendant of the historic Long family of Williamsville, original owners of the Williamsville Cemetery.
John Snyder	Son of Jacob and Fanny Snyder.
Benjamin Snyder	Son of Jacob and Fanny Snyder, husband of Susanna Fogelsonger.
Susanna (Fogelsonger) Snyder	Wife of Benjamin Snyder.
Fogelsonger Memorial	A prominent family in both Snyder and Williamsville, the family operated the

quarry on Main Street and Fogelsonger Road (now Park Club Lane) and fielded a musical group that would frequent Snyder's band hall.

Landel Memorial — A prominent family in both Snyder and Williamsville, the Landels owned a home building/construction business.

Charles Landel — Son of Julianna and Fred Landel, husband of Irene and owner of Landel Home Builders, Charles also served on the board of the Bank of Williamsville/Permanent Savings Bank.

Irene (Schoelles) Landel — Wife of Charles Landel and mother of Dorothy Shaver and Lois Fiddler.

Julianna Landel — Wife of Fred and mother of Charles and the author's namesake. Julianna and her daughter lived in Charles's Harlem Road house while his family lived in the garage.

Fred Landel — Father of Charles and husband of Julianna, Fred's family once lived in a white house on Main Street across from Getzville Road.

Cora (Landel) Gramm — Daughter of Julianna and Fred Landel.

Charles Fry — A gatekeeper of the Main Street Tollgate, Charles once chased a gate-crasher on horseback all the way to Williamsville just to collect the toll.

Frank Fry — A gatekeeper of the Main Street Tollgate and employee of the Hamlin estate.

Benjamin Fry — Father of Charles and Frank and a gatekeeper of the Main Street Tollgate.

Mary Fry — Mother of Charles and Frank and a gatekeeper of the Main Street Tollgate.

Tobias Witmer — Owner of a large Snyder farm and a schoolteacher at the Snyder School #18.

Elijah Long — A member of the prestigious Long family who presided as gatekeeper of the Main Street Tollgate.

Cemetery Section A *(right rear section)*

Hopkins Memorial
: One of the first families to live in Snyder, the Hopkinses went on to become a prestigious family in the politics and development of Snyder, Williamsville and the town of Amherst at large.

Timothy Hopkins
: Husband of Nancy Kerr and one of Snyder's earliest residents. Hopkins was a brigadier general during the War of 1812 and the first supervisor of the town of Amherst.

Nancy (Kerr) Hopkins
: Became the wife of Timothy in the first recorded marriage in Erie County. The Hopkins family originally lived on a plantation spanning the distance between our current Amherstdale Road and Washington Highway.

Cemetery Section E *(left rear section)*

Beulah (Snyder) Fiddler
: Wife of Earl, mother of Robert and Ruth and daughter of Solomon and Caroline Snyder, Beulah was married in the backyard of the Snyder band hall. After a series of moves, the Fiddlers moved into her Uncle Abraham Snyder's house at the corner of Main Street and Chateau. Beulah's diaries and photo albums provided much material for this book.

Earl Fiddler
: Husband of Beulah Snyder and father of Robert and Ruth.

Robert Fiddler
: Father of Julianna Fiddler-Woite, husband of Lois Landel and son of Earl and Beulah, Bob was a funeral director who served on the board of the Williamsville Cemetery.

REFERENCES

BOOKS

Bahr, Robert. *The Blizzard*. N.p.: Prentice-Hall, 1980.

Brown, R., and B. Watson. *Buffalo: Lake City in Niagara Land*. Windsor: USA, 1981.

Eberle, S., and J. Grande. *Second Looks: A Pictorial History of Buffalo and Erie County*. Virginia Beach, VA: Donning Co., 1987.

Gardner, H. *Art Through the Ages*. New York: Harcourt, Brace & World, Inc., 1959.

Grande, Joseph. *Glancing Back: A Pictorial History of Amherst, New York*. Virginia Beach, VA: Donning Co., 2000.

———. *Images of America: Amherst*. Charleston, SC: Arcadia Publishing, 2004.

Miller-Young, S. *History of the Town of Amherst*. N.p.: 1965.

Rossi, Erno. *White Death: The Blizzard of '77*. Canada: Seventy Seven Publishing, 1999.

NEWSPAPERS

Amherst Bee
Audubon Topics
Buffalo News
Buffalo Sunday Times

REFERENCES

INTERVIEWS AND DIARIES

Duax, Caroline
Fiddler, Beulah (Snyder)
Fiddler, Lois (Landel)
Fiddler, Robert
Hunt, Viola (Wannenwetsch)
Landel, Mary
McNeill, James
Merrill, Thomas
Quinn, Martin
Sawyer, Jane (Landel)
Shaver, Dorothy (Landel)
Shaver, William

WEBSITES

http://www.amherstcommunitychurch.org
http://www.charleslebrun.com
http://www.ctksnyder.com/church.htm
http://www.daemen.edu
http://www.erh.noaa.gov/er/buf/blizzard/bliz_stories.html
http://www.snyderfd.com/history.htm
http://www.theparkschool.org
http://www.wbuf.noaa.gov/bzpns.htm

Visit us at
www.historypress.net